THE
INTENTIONAL
FATHER

THE
INTENTIONAL
FATHER

A PRACTICAL GUIDE
to Raise Sons of
Courage AND Character

··· JON TYSON ···

BakerBooks

a division of Baker Publishing Group
Grand Rapids, Michigan

Text © 2021 by Jon Tyson
Research © 2021 by Barna Group

Published by Baker Books
a division of Baker Publishing Group
PO Box 6287, Grand Rapids, MI 49516-6287
www.bakerbooks.com

Printed in the United States of America

Library of Congress Cataloging-in-Publication Data
Names: Tyson, Jon, author.
Title: The intentional father : a practical guide to raise sons of courage and
    character / Jon Tyson.
Description: Grand Rapids, Michigan : Baker Books, a division of Baker
    Publishing Group, [2021] | Includes bibliographical references.
Identifiers: LCCN 2020039109 | ISBN 9780801018688 (cloth)
Subjects: LCSH: Fathers and sons—Religious aspects—Christianity. |
    Parenting—Religious aspects—Christianity. | Child rearing—Religious
    aspects—Christianity.
Classification: LCC BV4529.17 .T97 2021 | DDC 248.8/421—dc23
LC record available at https://lccn.loc.gov/2020039109

Interior design by William Overbeeke.

Baker Publishing Group publications use paper produced from sustainable forestry practices and post-consumer waste whenever possible.

23   24   25   26   27   28   10   9   8

For my father,

Ian Tyson,

whose prayers have carried me this far.

CONTENTS

FOREWORD

DAVID KINNAMAN,

president of Barna and aspiring intentional father

I ENCOUNTER QUESTIONS like these all the time: "Do you have any research or insights about raising boys?" "Why is it so hard to disciple young men?" "What can we do to make a real difference in the lives of our sons?"

I believe that answering these questions—thinking through the nature of the challenges they represent and turning our hearts, minds, and hands to solutions—is one of the urgent matters for Christians today.

Here's why: based on my Barna team's research, I contend that our society is facing a crisis of raising boys into men of character and consequence—that is, young men who live with integrity and make a positive impact with their lives. Whether we're talking about the powerful allure of video games and entertainment, the harmful forces of toxic masculinity, major disruptions to finding a vocation and work, questions of sex and sexuality (including queries into the nature of gender identity itself), the phenomenon of digital-access porn, the paucity of good role models for young men, or so much more, the obstacles seem stacked against young men. Not to mention the many roadblocks and speed bumps on the path to a young man "owning" his faith in today's spiritual ecosystem where young men—and young women too—are evangelized by the gospel according to YouTube.

It's easy to feel overwhelmed and that things are spinning out of your control. (Tip: they are.)

But there *is* a way forward. This remarkable book from my friend Jon Tyson is the field guide for walking the path of intentional fatherhood.

Now, beyond my profession as a social researcher and cultural analyst, I find the posture and practices Jon explores here to be deeply personal for me. I have struggled to know how to raise my own son, Zack Kinnaman, into a young man of character and consequence. Not because Zack isn't a great kid; he is. It just feels like the cultural deck is stacked against him, and against me as his dad. I've also seen other fathers in my close-knit circle of family and friends fight to form their sons into men of integrity and impact. The questions I mentioned at the start of this foreword? I hear them professionally *and* personally: in my work, in my friendships, and in my own soul.

And too often, as you'll see throughout this book, churches aren't helping us fathers find a better way. Barna's research for this project shows that practicing Christians are thinking about and experiencing fatherhood in much the same way as everyone else. Uncertain. Overwhelmed. Trying their best but not sure they're making a difference.

This is where the crisis of raising young men intersects this book. Jon is one of the most helpful voices from whom I've learned in my journey as a father. I have benefited from his disciplined intention around fatherhood through, for example, his terrific digital course called "The Primal Path" that undergirds this book. Truth is, I kept calling him for advice and then, after hours of anguished conversations, urged him to partner with us to make his insights more broadly available. The book you're holding is the result.

Jon is one of just a handful of men who have told me, without a hint of pride or puffery, that raising his son is one of the things he's gotten right. Think of that: I've met thousands of fathers, but only a handful of these have made it a *primary* ambition to be an intentional presence in the lives of their children and are willing to go on the record to say so. Imagine if the volume of fathers *intending to be intentional* was turned way up, aiming at nothing less than getting it right: we'd be miles ahead in solving this dilemma.

This book aims to help you aim higher.

I can hear the objections that may flood your thinking. What about mothers? Don't they matter too? Of course! A thousand times, yes! This book is particularly written to give lessons to fathers, but it also has wisdom for moms and women who are the guardians of sons (and daughters). Jon made an intentional decision—and we supported it—to focus on helping dads like me. And the Barna team made a similar determination to focus our research lens on the plight of raising young men, even though many of our research-based insights also apply to shaping girls into young women of character and consequence. (What I've learned has absolutely helped me in raising my daughters, Emily and Annika.)

But trying to solve everything often results in nothing at all, so *this* book looks specifically at becoming an intentional father to address the particular, vexing challenges of raising sons of consequence.

My friendship with Zack has blossomed over the last year. His curiosity and strength inspire me, and our closeness forms a deep well of resilience for us both. I still have so much to learn, but with Jon's help, I'm convinced that, in working to become an intentional father, I have entered into something truly sacred. I pray this book will help you experience some of the deepest joys you can imagine with your son, as I have with mine.

ACKNOWLEDGMENTS

THANKS TO MY SON, Nathan, for the privilege and joy of walking closely through these complex, deep, and meaningful years. It was your life that inspired me to try to become an intentional father.

A NOTE *to the* READER

WITHIN THIS BOOK are principles primarily geared toward raising sons. I focus on ways we can intentionally raise young men for three main reasons: First, I compiled this material over many years while attempting to become an intentional father for my own son, Nate, and when I was putting it all together, I had him in mind. Second, these teachings were also used in a video series I called "The Primal Path," which was specifically designed to help fathers of sons. Third, our culture has done a terrible job raising young men, and there is a huge need for formational instruction that will help fathers, and other guardians of young men, intentionally bring their sons from boyhood into manhood.

I highly encourage you to engage in these practices even if, or maybe especially if, your situation isn't "normal" (whatever that means). Maybe you're a stepdad trying to forge a relationship with a stepson; maybe you're the guardian of a boy who is not your biological son; maybe you're divorced and trying to manage parenting part-time or from a distance; maybe you have more than one son; maybe you're a mentor.

The point is, this book is for all father figures, even those of us going through various hardships or limiting circumstances. Engage where you can, do what you can, and make all the difference you can. I am confident this book will help you create young men of consequence.

With the current epidemic of toxic masculinity, the rapid emergence of damage revealed by the #metoo movement, and the breakdown in relationships between fathers and sons, the young men in our care are at a crucial time in history. The pressures on them are great. But so too is their potential.

A generation of intentional fathers will turn the tide.

PART 1

...

INTRODUCTION

"How are you going to live
in the world?" he asked his son.
"Tell me that. How are you going
to be a man and live in the world?"

• • •

NIALL WILLIAMS, *The Fall of Light*

CHAPTER ONE

There Is a Need for Fathers

He will turn the hearts of the parents to their children, and the hearts of the children to their parents; or else I will come and strike the land with total destruction.

MALACHI 4:6

Any fool can have a child. That doesn't make you a father. It's the courage to raise a child that makes you a father.

BARACK OBAMA

THE PRINCIPLE

The role of fatherhood is one of the most overlooked yet crucial roles in our society. The data and our own experience could not be clearer. When a father is present, emotionally healthy, and involved in his child's life, the child has a tremendous advantage in the world to navigate its complexities and challenges with joy and confidence.

I STOOD BESIDE MY WIFE in the doctor's office as the ultrasound technician ran the wand over her stomach. The room was silent, and I gave my wife's hand a squeeze. Christy and I had gotten married in our early twenties, and she had become pregnant before we celebrated our first anniversary. Looking back, it seems to me like we were just kids sitting there, so young, waiting for the news.

The tech turned to us with a smile on her face and asked the question we had both been waiting for.

"Do you want to know the sex of your child?"

We looked at each other, grinning nervously, and Christy nodded.

This was the big moment.

"Yeah," I said. "Go on." I could feel the blood rushing in my ears.

"Okay," the technician said. "Well, congratulations! It's a boy!"

It's a boy.

And with those words, a feeling washed over me that I hadn't expected—not joy or relief or excitement. I wasn't thinking of teaching my son sports someday or what it would be like to go to a concert with him. I wasn't looking forward to showing him how to ride a bike or taking him camping.

No, the primary thing I felt in that moment was overwhelming anxiety.

How will I ever have what it takes to be the kind of father my son needs?

How will I teach him all the things he needs to know?

How will I not let him down?

AT AGE TWENTY-TWO I felt suddenly thrust into being an adult. Did you experience a similar moment?

I left that doctor's appointment in a complete state of shock and drove back to the butcher shop at Albertson's where I worked. I stared ahead through my car's windshield and tried not to contemplate the enormity of the task at hand.

Raising a son.

That was one of the most sobering drives of my entire life. Even after returning to work, I couldn't stop thinking about this baby boy soon to come into the world. He would look to me to find a model of manhood and would in many ways derive his image of God from our relationship. I wasn't sure I was ready for that. I wasn't convinced I had been raised properly—how could I possibly have the necessary tools and knowledge to raise a son in a God-honoring way?

I doubted I had what it took.

But none of that changed anything. I was going to have a son, ready or not, and he would be arriving in a few short months.

My anxiety didn't diminish in those months. In fact, it only increased, and before I knew it, the time came for my son to arrive.

There in the delivery room, moments after he was born, the nurse handed me my son. Nathan. He was beautiful. I was beaming with pride for him and for what Christy had done. I was a father—what a feeling!

Yet, even then, the same doubts raced through my mind.

I don't know if I'm going to be able to raise this boy.

Do I have what it takes?

Have you ever doubted your ability as a father?

This concept of "raising" a child comes to us from a rather intense tradition rooted in Roman culture. Children were presented before the head of the household, and if the father wanted the child, he would lift the baby up in his arms and

About the Data in This Book

Throughout *The Intentional Father* you'll find stats, charts, and other data visualizations based on new Barna research among U.S. fathers of children, teens, or young adults ages ten to twenty-five. Most feature data from a nationally representative group of 1,058 dads from across America (you can read more about Barna's survey methodology in the "About the Research" chapter), but faith-related questions look deeper at a group of 612 fathers we call "practicing Christians." These Christians have attended a worship service within the past month and strongly agree that faith is very important in their lives. Wherever you fall on the faith spectrum, there are fathers just like you who are doing their best to parent on purpose.

hold him or her skyward—literally raising the child—and this meant the baby was welcomed into the home. If the man didn't want the child, he would not raise him or her but would look away and leave the baby there on the ground, and then the child was put out for what they called "exposure."

We take this phrase for granted, this raising of a son, but it's a heavy term, isn't it? When we say we're raising a child, what we're actually communicating, based on the history of the phrase, is, "I want you. I want you in my life. I'm going to take responsibility for you, and I'm going to give you everything I can to help you grow up and mature into the best person you can be."

So how do we raise a boy into manhood in this day and age? How can we raise a child into adulthood during these difficult times?

You've probably searched out this book because you, like me when I realized a son was on the way, feel overwhelmed at the prospect of raising a child into adulthood. Let me tell you this: you're not alone. I've actually met very few men who, when it comes to raising their kids, feel well equipped. I've met very few men who, when confronted with the knowledge that they are having a baby, swell up with confidence that they have the skills and tools needed to raise this tiny child all the way up into adulthood.

But while I don't meet a lot of men who are confident, I do meet a lot of men who are determined. You're reading this book, so this is probably you.

You're determined to get it right.

You're determined to pass on a legacy of blessing instead of brokenness.

You're determined to raise a child of consequence.

And because of that determination, because of that desire, I want to affirm you and honor you for your willingness to do the work, for looking around, and for trying to figure out how to raise your child in a God-honoring way.

You're already on the right path.

Raising young men properly is a huge need in our culture right now. Just look around. We're living in a time where men don't know what it means to be men anymore, and women don't know what it means to be women. It feels to me like there is total confusion. It's hard enough to simply grow up into some kind of a functional human being, much less set out on a journey to discover what it means to be a man. What it means to be an adult.

At the heart of our culture's inability to raise boys into men is an epidemic of fatherlessness. Here are just a few stats relating to how the absence of fathers is impacting our society, from fatherhood.org.[1] Children without fathers:

» are four times more likely to live in poverty.
» are more likely to suffer emotional and behavioral problems.

- » have higher levels of aggressive behavior than children born into married homes.
- » have two times the risk of infant mortality.
- » are more likely to go to prison. Only one in five prison inmates grew up with their father present.
- » are twice as likely to be involved in early sexual activity.

WHAT A HEARTBREAKING FORECAST for sons and daughters who are not raised by their fathers. Your willingness to step up is an incredibly important thing, and it's going to leave a legacy, not only in the life of your son but also in the flourishing of your community, the advancement of your nation, and even the thriving of our world.

This is a huge deal.

Still, there are some things we need to clarify before we can move forward, and they have to do with the concept of manhood. There is a lot of confusion in our culture surrounding that, and rightly so. After all, the behavior of our present generation of men has stirred all kinds of questions and doubts to the surface.

What are we going to do about toxic masculinity, and how does that come into this journey we're about to embark on?

Everyone sees the results of broken masculinity and so is naturally leery of a book like this one that calls men into masculinity, into manhood. Many people equate our current broken example with true masculinity itself, and so they think masculinity needs to be done away with. In their experience, "masculinity" has led to abuse, pain, and unhealthy hierarchies that diminish women. It has led to the prevalence of rape culture on campuses, the pornification of our lives, and the need for the #metoo movement, a crucial tide change exposing the broken side of masculinity in our culture.

It's easy to see why masculinity has a bad rap.

But healthy masculinity does none of those things. True masculinity has the strength to smash hierarchies, stand up for those on the margins, and lead men into lives where they are stopping abuse from happening.

How can we do this? How can we raise our sons into healthy masculinity, into a God-honoring way of being a man?

Maybe you're watching your son grow up, you realize he's about to enter his teenage years, and a sense of panic is filling your heart. You've seen this coming for quite a while, but now the time is upon you, and you're overwhelmed by what you haven't yet done and what you still hope to do before your son leaves the house. If you're anything like I was, you're wondering if there is some kind of initiation, some sort of path for you and your son to follow. But when you look around, you realize that, for the most part, these kinds of meaningful ceremonies have been stripped away from our modern society.

How do you measure the precise time your son enters into the path of manhood? How will you know when your son has

Prepared for Parenthood?

Half of all U.S. dads say they did *not* feel fully prepared for fatherhood before their child came into the world. However, practicing Christian fathers are a bit more likely than the national average to say they felt very prepared.

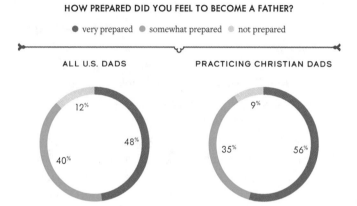

HOW PREPARED DID YOU FEEL TO BECOME A FATHER?

● very prepared   ● somewhat prepared   ● not prepared

ALL U.S. DADS

12%
48%
40%

PRACTICING CHRISTIAN DADS

9%
35%
56%

n=562 U.S. fathers 18 and older, *n*=612 U.S. practicing Christian fathers 18 and older, May 2020. Practicing Christians have attended a worship service within the past month and strongly agree that faith is very important in their lives.

become a man? Is it when he turns eighteen or twenty-one? Gets married? Is it when he loses his virginity? Gets drunk for the first time? Graduates from college? Is it when he gets his driver's license or when someone older than him tells him he's a man? In almost every other culture, there is a codified, intentional, intense pathway to develop adolescents into adults. But in Western, U.S. culture, there's almost nothing.

Author Ronald Rolheiser talks about the dangers of this apparent lack of initiation. He admits that some of the initiation rites of primitive cultures can seem intense. After all, in a few of the more brutal ones, young men would actually die striving to attain manhood. We look at that today, and we think, *How barbaric! How could we do that to our young people? How could we ask them to go through something so ferocious?*

But Rolheiser goes on to ask an important question: "Do you know what's really killing our young people today?"[2]

The answer is self-initiation.

When there's no older generation intentionally ushering boys into manhood, when there's no tribe of mentors or fathers taking their sons along a predetermined path, many of our young men try to establish themselves, attempting to walk through the wilderness of adolescence with the hope that, somehow, they'll find their way into adulthood on their own.

But look around and you'll see where this self-initiation is getting us.

Look at the rates of teen pregnancy and STDs and violence.

Look at the number of young people engaged in self-harm.

Look at the suicide rates.

Look at the rape culture on our college campuses and the porn addiction epidemic.

Young men, while attempting to self-initiate their way into manhood, are actually carrying their adolescence into adulthood.

We are surrounded by adult men who, in actuality, are nothing more than teenagers, still trying to find their way, hurting and abusing those around them, all while thinking it's some kind of amusing game.

What our young men are really saying is, "Here I am! I'm growing up! I'm emerging! Will someone please take my hand and walk me through this time of confusion?"

As a generation, in many ways, we have turned our backs on them. And so, I determined in my heart that I would not turn my back on my son.

You're reading this book, so you must have made the same resolution.

The first question we have to explore is, What kind of father are you?

QUESTIONS *to* Think About

☞ What comes to your mind when you hear the word *masculinity*?

☞ What are some of the key moments in your life that forged you into the man you are today? What did you learn from them? How can you prepare to pass them on?

INTENTIONALSTEPS

What age is your son right now? What do you need to do to prepare him for the journey into manhood he is about to embark on?

CHAPTER TWO

Five Kinds of Fathers

Boys do not long for fathers who will usher them through the gauntlet of psychological disconnect. They long for fathers who have themselves survived intact. Boys do not ache for their father's masculinity. They ache for their fathers' hearts.

T-REAL

THE PRINCIPLE

Being a father is one of the most sacred responsibilities a man can have. The current crisis among fathers threatens to destroy

*this generation. Stepping up and becoming intentional fathers
will confront this brokenness and leave a powerful legacy in the
lives of our sons.*

DID YOU KNOW there are five types of fathers out
there? Which of the following types best describes
you?

There is the *irresponsible father*, one who has literally zero
involvement with his kids, someone who completely bails
on them to the point that they don't even know who he is.
This father takes no responsibility, provides no child support, and contributes no meaningful support into the lives
of his children.

Then there is the *ignorant father*. This type of father has
no idea what he's doing and continually wreaks havoc in the
lives of his children without even realizing it. He doesn't
know anything about being a father, and he doesn't try to
learn or improve. Because of all of this, he ends up projecting
his own brokenness into the lives of his children.

There is the *inconsistent father* who is torn by personal ambition. He has the capability of doing better at this fathering
thing, but instead he prioritizes his own job, career, and hobbies. These binges of selfishness are often followed by guilt
and feeble attempts to fix everything, but there is no stable
sense of security or identity passed down to his children.

There is the *involved father*. This type of dad shows up at
sporting events and takes the time to put porn filters on his

kids' devices. He gets a lot of things right, but because of the business of life and the failure to ask the right questions, he never seeks to understand specifically who his children are and why God gave them to him. This is a noble dad, but one haunted by the sense that there is something more, another layer or level in his parenting.

Then there is the intentional father.

The *intentional father* is deeply invested in discovering who his children are and how he can help them reach their redemptive potential. He seeks to understand the children God has given him and wants to form them into young persons who can fulfill their purpose. He sees parenting as central to his call before God and does it with all of his might. This kind of father leaves multigenerational blessing in the lives of his children.

This book is all about becoming that fifth kind of father.

Again I ask, Which type are you? Be honest.

Are you willing to put in the time required to become an intentional father and help your children thrive?

THERE IS ONE SEGMENT of the United States population that seems to have a good handle on what it takes to raise young men, and they even have a path in place to facilitate it. I saw it firsthand in my twenties when I was a youth pastor in Franklin, Tennessee, at a wonderful church. Part of my responsibilities there involved running campus ministries, and I spent a lot of time at colleges with a handful of my student leaders. I was consciously struck by the quality of this one group of young people; they seemed to be a little more rooted than everyone else and a lot more stable.

When I bumped into any one of these kids, I'd introduce myself and ask questions. There had to be a reason they were adjusting to adulthood better than everyone else. And repeatedly I got the same answer.

"Hi!" they would say. "I'm a Mormon, in the Church of Jesus Christ of Latter-Day Saints."

After this happened numerous times, I asked myself, *What are the Mormons doing that we're not doing?* Now, I understood that the Jewish community had bar mitzvahs and a process to help their young men emerge into adulthood, and Roman Catholics and mainline Protestant churches had catechism, but those were primarily faith mechanisms. What were the Mormons doing to bring their young people into this all-encompassing, confident adulthood?

I had to find out, so I reached out to a local Mormon leader, and in talking to him I realized the Mormons had a very, very intentional pathway for the formation of their young men.

The first thing I noticed was the mindset they try to instill into every single young man: they want them to be infused with a sense of priesthood. As boys enter adolescence, they are given a sense that they are part of the spiritual authority of the church and bear responsibility for its ongoing health.

Part of this is a thing they call seminary, where for an hour every day before school, all Mormon young people go to a study where they learn and grow in their faith. They study the Old Testament one year and the New Testament another year, go through the Doctrine and Covenants and the Pearl of Great Price, and ultimately study the Book of Mormon.

After all of that comes the final step of initiation, probably one you've seen yourself—they send primarily the young men on a two-year mission around the world to spread the Mormon gospel, and you can imagine how formative that experience must be, what a liminal space that must create, and how transforming it is. At the end of those two years, they're officially welcomed home, back into the larger Mormon society, and they're recognized for the journey they've been on.

Now, I'm not Mormon, but as I heard more about the path they provided for their young people, a question began to formulate in my mind, one that would set me on a quest unlike anything I'd ever embarked on before. That question was, *How can I put something like this in place for my son?*

I started out on a journey of discovery.

This was the biggest, most comprehensive thing I had undertaken in my life. I read every book you've ever heard of in regard to manhood, not just in the Christian tradition but from a whole range of perspectives. I was determined to find out what it meant to be a man, what the role of manhood was, and how I could guide my son into that space of healthy, God-honoring masculinity.

I began when my son was very small, so that I'd have plenty of time to try to figure out a good way forward. *The Intentional Father* is what came out of that exploration. Let me also say that I'm not some kind of expert in the field. I don't have degrees in childhood development or cultural studies. I'm not a social worker or a statistician. But this material has been field-tested by many, many fathers, and I've put a lot of time into it. I've worked really hard to clarify the core elements needed to raise healthy and functional men.

My advice as you read this book is to take what works for you, innovate on it, and build it out for yourself. Adjust it as you would like for your daughters too—I stand by the principles in the book, and many apply to young women as well as young men. I simply hope this book gives you a good jumping-off point, a place to start on your quest to become an intentional father.

BEFORE WE GO too much further, it's important we solidify one thing: What is the definition of a man?

This is in many ways the story of my journey with Nate, and if you want to help your son become a man, it seems rather important to have at least a passing understanding of the place you're trying to take him.

Here's my take: *a man is an image bearer and son of God entrusted with power and the responsibility to create, cultivate, care, and defend, for God's glory and the good of others.*

As we move forward with this definition of manhood and masculinity—how a man relates to God and who he is in the world—we will be operating between two guardrails, two things I think are crucial to keep in mind during the entire journey of being an intentional father: *submission* and *servanthood*.

Adam, the first man, failed in his responsibilities with God and others because of two things. The first was rebellion and the second was laziness. He wanted to go his own way, and when that didn't work out, he refused to accept responsibility. I want to see godly men operating with authority and responsibility, living for the glory of God and the good of others and submitting to God and serving others. If we can keep those things in mind, they will provide a nice framework for moving forward as an intentional father.

You see, ultimately, my conviction as a follower of Jesus is that we are called to help our sons become like Jesus. My vision is not to produce men who conform to a list of traits that cause the world to say, "Now that's a man!" My goal is to help our sons become like Jesus. It's what my goal was for my son when I started out on this path, and that's still my goal.

Why? Because Jesus was the best man who ever lived. Look at his life, his cause, his compassion, his courage, his love for other people, his walk with his heavenly Father, his willingness to confront hypocrisy, his personal integrity. When you look at the life of Jesus, you can say that he got it right in every single situation he was in. That's what the vision of being an intentional father is—to help our sons become like Jesus.

I started my son down this path from boyhood to manhood when he was thirteen, and after five years he went off on his gap year, getting ready for the rest of his life. And people who I know or who saw our journey unfolding on social media often asked, "What did you do? What did you read? What was the framework? What rituals did you do, and what process did you go through?"

That's what I want to share with you. That's what we're going to spend the rest of our time talking through: how to create a robust, multiyear journey to take your son through, a journey at the end of which you can both confidently say he has become a man, ready to live out the rest of his life.

WHILE I WAS WALKING with my son, Nate, down this path, we had a daily ritual where we would sit down and have time together in the mornings. It was a discipleship meeting—we basically woke up early and drank coffee together.

After about two years of doing this, Nate stopped in the middle of one of our sessions and said to me, "Dad, where did all of this come from?"

"What do you mean?" I asked him.

He paused. "I mean, who took you through this program? Where did you learn all this stuff about manhood? Who helped you get it in your life?"

I sat there silently, thinking through his question.

The truth was, no one had done this with me.

"No one poured into my life like this," I explained quietly. "I made this whole thing up for you. I did it because I love you, I care about you, and I have a vision for who you can be in the world. I made this program for you because I want you to be a man of consequence."

It was an extraordinary moment. Tears filled his eyes.

"Wow, Dad," he said in a hushed voice. "I feel really, really loved."

What else can you hope other than that your son understands, deep in his heart, that you love him? That you're pouring into him because of how much you care about him and the life he is going to lead?

You will have moments like this, where your child has a sudden realization about how much you love him. In those moments, he will say the same thing to you. "Thank you, Dad, for leaving me a legacy. Thank you, Dad, for pouring into me. Thank you, Dad, for caring about me enough to spend the time, energy, and resources to help me become a good and godly man."

Before we really dig in, I want to clarify briefly what *The Intentional Father* is and what it isn't. It is a discipleship and formation pathway to walk through with your son, beginning in his adolescence and continuing through his entry into adulthood. It is both comprehensive and customizable, which means there may be a few things you choose to do a bit differently than I did, and there might be things you want to insert or remove.

Here's what it isn't. I'm not going to disciple your son for you. I don't have downloadable daily devotions for you to read together, and I did this on purpose, because your son

A Man with a Plan for Raising His Kids

Most dads say they have at least the outlines of a plan for how to raise young men or women—but half or fewer *strongly* agree, indicating a lot of opportunity to get more intentional.

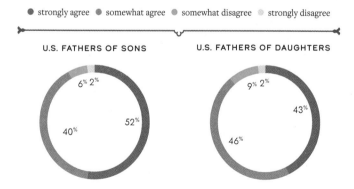

"I HAVE A PLAN FOR HOW TO GUIDE, TRAIN, AND TEACH MY SON/DAUGHTER TO BECOME A MAN/WOMAN."

● strongly agree ● somewhat agree ● somewhat disagree ● strongly disagree

U.S. FATHERS OF SONS

6% 2%
52%
40%

U.S. FATHERS OF DAUGHTERS

9% 2%
43%
46%

n=451 U.S. fathers of sons, *n=413* U.S. fathers of daughters, May 2020.

is not my son. He is probably very different from my son. I'll provide some potential resources, some things that were very helpful for me, but it will still be up to you to grow as a father in knowing your son and discerning what he needs. And I want you to grow as a follower of Jesus and deepen your own faith as you go along.

Maybe you're reading this entirely of your own accord, or maybe someone bought this for you or passed it on to you. Maybe you're a stepdad or a single mom or an uncle or a mentor or a sibling to a young man, and you're rising up to fill in this gap where a father is missing. Maybe you're wondering, *Is this going to work for me?*

Yes, this will work for you. Own it, tweak it, customize it, and do not listen to the lie that, because this young man isn't your biological son or you're not his biological father, you can't speak into his life and this journey won't change his life for the good. Reject those doubts. You can have an incredible impact on the life of the person you are trying to invest in.

Others of you might have different doubts. Maybe you're thinking, *Jon, are you trying to feed into gender stereotypes here? What do you think about transgender boys, or what if my son is gay? Will this work for him?*

Those are difficult, complicated questions. But the most important thing in all of this is to love and pour into your son. No effort of love, discipleship, and development will ever be wasted in the life of your son, regardless of who he is or what he is wrestling with.

Don't worry about stereotypes. I'm also not trying to produce a generation of alpha males. But I do believe there are distinct differences between men and women, and that God designed us to work in partnership with one another. A big part of our current crisis is that men don't know who they need to be around women. I believe that fathers mentoring their sons in the way I am about to describe will benefit our culture.

Let's wrap up this chapter with our first two exercises, the first being an exercise of fasting and prayer. I want to encourage you to do at least a twenty-four-hour fast and to devote that time to prayer, asking God for wisdom, grace, and perseverance, and that you'd have a heart to pour into your son and walk with him along this path.

I believe if you take the time to do this, God will speak to you about your own heart and about your son, and you'll have the spiritual covering to begin to move into this and start this conversation with your son. Beginning with a dedicated time of prayer and fasting will set a beautiful trajectory for what's to come.

The second exercise is to watch the documentary *The Work*. *The Work* is one of the most visceral films I've ever seen, and I've watched a lot of documentaries. This is one about men in Folsom Prison who are dealing with their brokenness, much of it from their childhoods. Many of the deep issues they explore are the very things that led to their incarceration and resulted in so much of the pain they're experiencing.

This film also documents the first time outsiders, folks from regular society, were invited into the prison to do a shared group session.

Why should I watch this? you might wonder. Because this documentary will show you the incredibly high stakes we're talking about when it comes to raising our sons through these vital years. Sure, it shows guys living in prison and reveals the lack of father figures in their lives, and that might be the motivation you need to become a better leader for your son.

But what I'm really focused on in this documentary are the guys who visit the prisoners. That's what woke me up. These stoic, emotionally removed men (pretty typical in our culture) are brought to tears when they begin exploring the things that have affected them in their own lives.

So, spend some time in prayer and fasting, watch *The Work*, let God do a deep work in your heart, and then you'll be ready to jump into the next chapter.

QUESTIONS *to* Think About

☞ What emotions rose in you when your kids were born?

☞ Which of the five fathers best describes how you have acted?

☞ Reflect back on your own adolescence. What moments with your father shaped your life?

☞ What are you hoping to see in your relationship with your son as a result of reading and implementing the things in this book?

☞ What fears or hesitations do you have?

INTENTIONALSTEPS

Do a twenty-four-hour fast and dedicate that time to prayer. Write down the things that come to mind about how you were fathered and the kind of father you would like to be. Offer the years ahead to God, and ask for help in what's to come. And watch the documentary *The Work*.

PART 2

PREPARATION

Before Dads Became Fathers, They Were Sons

Barna researchers asked today's dads to reflect on their relationship with their own father or father figure, both during childhood and now as an adult. How would they characterize that bond—or lack thereof? Most, about three-quarters, would call it *excellent* or *good*. The remaining adult sons' descriptions run the gamut from *fair* to *we didn't/don't have a relationship*.

U.S. DADS RATE THEIR RELATIONSHIP WITH THEIR OWN FATHER, THEN AND NOW

How would you describe your overall relationship with your father (or father figure)?

● excellent ● good ● fair ○ poor/very poor
○ complicated ● we didn't/don't have a relationship

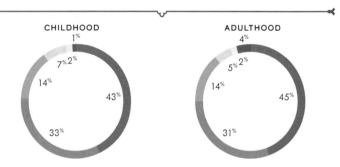

CHILDHOOD

1%
7% 2%
14%
43%
33%

ADULTHOOD

4%
5% 2%
14%
45%
31%

Regardless of how they portray their father-son relationship, a majority (85%) say their father figure's impact on their own ability to be a good dad has been positive—even if that means, in the words of one respondent, "by showing me what *not* to do." However, in a separate Barna study of men's self-perceptions and well-being, data analysts found that Christian dads who report a positive father-son relationship while growing up are more likely to be very satisfied (53%) with their relationship with their own child, compared with those whose father-son relationship was not positive (42%).* So there's strong indication—maybe even in ways we're not aware of—that Dad matters.

n=542 U.S. fathers 18 and older who had a father or father figure during childhood, *n*=396 U.S. fathers 18 and older who have a father or father figure who is still living, May 2020.
Five Essentials to Engage Today's Men: Conversations Every Church Should Have about How Men Connect with Their Purpose, with Others & with Their Faith (Ventura, CA: Barna Group, 2020).

Researchers gave adult sons a chance to describe their father's parenting in their own words—the good, the bad, and, for a few, the downright ugly. Larger words or phrases indicate themes highlighted by a greater percentage of respondents.

WHAT MY DAD GOT RIGHT

HE TAUGHT ME HOW TO DEFEND MYSELF, HOW TO FISH, AND HOW TO TREAT A LADY

on my side no matter what, always there for me

COOKING FOR US

SENSE OF HUMOR

good provider

LOVING

SERVANT'S HEART

nothing

HARDWORKING

HONEST   INVOLVED IN SPORTS

FUN!   loving,
supportive,
compassionate,
kind   STRICT

everything   OPEN-MINDED

TAUGHT US LIFE SKILLS

LOYAL   strong
work ethic

HE STAYED
MARRIED TO MOM   RESPONSIBLE

being a good role model

HE TAUGHT ME THE RIGHT LES-
SONS, EVEN IF AT THE TIME I
THOUGHT HE WAS WRONG

teaching me right from wrong

SHARED HIS LOVE OF RACING

FAITHFUL

WHAT MY DAD GOT WRONG

ONCE I TURNED 17, I NEVER
SAW HIM AGAIN

not being there for me

HE WAS HUMAN

too judgmental,
closed-minded

HE WORKED
TOO MUCH

HE DIDN'T LISTEN

nothing

PARTYING TOO MUCH

not very emotionally
involved, didn't show love,
lack of empathy

SELFISH DECISIONS

angry, mean,
abusive   TOO STRICT

HE WAS NOT ABLE TO GIVE GOOD
FINANCIAL OR CAREER ADVICE

addiction,
drank too much

TOO OLD-FASHIONED

DIVORCE

WHUPPING ME

CHEATED ON MY MOTHER

FORCED ME TO STRIVE
FOR HIS GOALS, NOT MY OWN

CHAPTER THREE

A Preview
of the Possible

It is easier to build strong children than to repair broken men.

FREDERICK DOUGLASS

THE PRINCIPLE

We need to have a vision of the day our sons will leave our homes and work backward from that day with a plan to help them gain the knowledge, skills, character, and experiences they need. This will enable them to move into the world as confident and healthy men.

THERE'S A MOMENT I need you to grapple with as a father. It's a moment that's coming for you—in fact, it's right around the corner, happening way sooner than you expect. And there's absolutely nothing you can do to stop it.

Know what that moment is?

It's the moment your son leaves your home.

One day, you're going to give him a hug, pat him on the shoulder, and watch as he walks out, be it on his way to college or to his first apartment. Maybe you'll be the one driving away, or maybe he'll be walking through a crowd on his way into an airport. Maybe he'll climb into an Uber or taxi.

That's when the questions will start pouring into your mind.

What have I given him?

What wisdom, what love, what lessons is he carrying into the world?

What brokenness is he bearing?

What is my legacy to him?

I remember very, very clearly the day I left my parents' house and moved to the United States to study theology. I packed everything I owned into two suitcases. I walked down the line of everyone I knew, shook their hands, looked them in the eye, and then walked through airport security. Right as I was about to turn the corner, I heard a woman cry out, very loud, and there was incredible pain in her voice.

"My son! My son!"

It was my mother, but I didn't turn around. I let out a heavy, shaky sigh, put on my headphones, and listened to the soundtrack from the movie *Braveheart* as I walked into my future. I know it might seem shocking to some, but for me, I was forsaking absolutely everything in order to build a new life. Later, my mom would tell me how proud she was of me when I walked away that day, starting out on my own.

All I took with me? Those two suitcases. They symbolized everything to me, all the lessons I had learned, the wisdom I had gained, my relationships with my father and grandfather. It was all there in those bags, one in each of my hands.

Your son is going to walk out into the world one day.

What will he take with him?

IN THE BOOK *The Seven Habits of Highly Effective People*, author Stephen Covey communicates a powerful concept called The Funeral Exercise.[1] It is an exercise in which you take a moment and imagine you're at a funeral. Everyone around you is sad. There are a lot of flowers. People are weeping and sharing thoughts about the person who died. They're standing up and affirming the deceased.

Then Covey lets you in on something. This funeral you're attending? It's your own.

In The Funeral Exercise, you are encouraged to ask specific questions: If this is your funeral, what do you want your spouse to say about you? What would you like to hear your kids say? What would you hope your coworkers would say? And, ultimately, what witness would God give on your one and only life?

That's a powerful exercise.

But there's another version of this, one that every father needs to prepare for and think through, and that's The Day Your Son Will Leave Home Exercise.

Most of us have a strong desire to send our sons into the world prepared, formed, and equipped. We want them to head out on their own with valuable resources and tools that will help them live the best life they can, be strong men of character, and point people to Jesus. This is true of just about every father out there, even those who on the surface might appear disinterested in their sons. The reality is that fathers have this desire for their children. It's ingrained.

But reality bumps up against this desire because we don't have a plan. The painful truth is that we really have no strategic way of seeing those wonderful dreams come to pass. This creates a sense of anxiety in us, a kind of dread, because we have this feeling that if we aren't more intentional about what we're doing, the only way our desires for our children will come to pass is through sheer luck.

And we don't want to depend on luck where our children are concerned.

There is good news: you can have a plan.

Start by thinking about the day your son leaves the house. Imagine it in detail. Where do you say goodbye to him? Do you give him a hug? Are you crying? Imagine that day, and then imagine the things you want him to take out into the world with him. What's in his suitcases?

A Man with a Plan for Making Disciples

On the whole, practicing Christian dads take discipleship seriously, and most see the connection between their fathering and their child growing into an adult Christ follower. However, a small but significant minority express some uncertainty in this area.

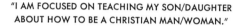

"I AM FOCUSED ON TEACHING MY SON/DAUGHTER ABOUT HOW TO BE A CHRISTIAN MAN/WOMAN."

● strongly agree ● somewhat agree ● somewhat disagree ○ strongly disagree

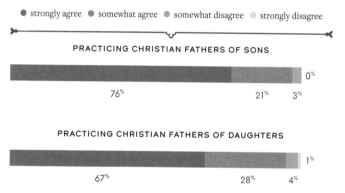

PRACTICING CHRISTIAN FATHERS OF SONS

76%   21%   3%   0%

PRACTICING CHRISTIAN FATHERS OF DAUGHTERS

67%   28%   4%   1%

n=520 U.S. practicing Christian fathers of sons, n=447 U.S. practicing Christian fathers of daughters, May 2020. Practicing Christians have attended a worship service within the past month and strongly agree that faith is very important in their lives.

This is where your specific plan for your specific child begins.

This day has already happened for me, and it was a tough one in our home, I'm not going to lie. On that particular morning, my son set his alarm for 5:30 a.m.; he packed everything he owned into two bags, and I walked him outside. We stood on the sidewalk outside of our New York City apartment. We hugged one another. I looked him in the eye. Then he climbed into his Uber and went to the airport.

He was gone.

He left home.

The day had come and gone.

But I had planned for it. And because I had planned for it, I had few regrets, no qualms, and very little anxiety. I felt good about what I had given him to take along on the journey. I had confidence he had the tools to cope with almost any situation.

You *can* feel that way when your child walks out the door—you just need to plan for it.

In order to get started, there are four questions I want you to think through so that when that day comes, you won't be left standing there, watching your son walk away and wondering why you didn't equip him the way he needed to be equipped.

> *What do you want your son to know about God, about himself, and about life?* This is essentially a question about wisdom. What do you want him to know? I'm sure there are particular views of God you'd like him to embrace, and it would be nice if he had a certain level of self-confidence as he walked out the door. So start thinking through what you want him to know in big, general terms.

Who do you want your son to be? There are all kinds of young men in the world—just look at the news, pay attention to professional athletics, or watch the workforce around you, and you'll quickly see the variety of young men making their way in the world. What sort of character do you want your son to exhibit, and how is that going to be formed in him? I can promise you this: character isn't developed by accident.

What skills do you want your son to have? There is nothing more frustrating for a young man than being sent out into the world only to be immediately confronted with practical things he doesn't know how to do. I'm talking about basic stuff here: how to change a tire, how to open a retirement account, the importance of writing a thank-you note. Start thinking about practical skills you've found useful in life, as well as things you wish someone would have taught you earlier.

What formational experiences do you want him to have? Ultimately, this is your responsibility: helping your son go out into the world with wisdom, character, skills—and with key experiences that have reinforced the first three.

Most fathers let chance take care of these things (or not). They leave it up to luck. Every so often they'll think of these questions in one form or another, but they push them away, hoping someone else will teach their son these things, or maybe they'll somehow learn them on their own. This is why most sons go out into the world only knowing what life just so happens to teach them, or developing the kind of character the world values, or gaining skills only in the heat of the moment, as needed.

But chance is a lousy teacher and an even worse guide.

Don't leave these things up to chance or fate or happenstance—be intentional.

Think about this now.

Somebody is going to disciple your son. Somebody is going to give your son wisdom on how to live, and it's either going to be you and a community of godly men (see exercise #3 below) or it's going to be the world. Your son is going to become someone—he is going to grow up. His character will be formed by someone.

Why not take responsibility and personally give him the key things he needs?

May it never be said that your son thinks there is more wisdom about life from Google and YouTube than from you. May it be said that you were the one who gave him the skills he needed and exposed him to other people who could teach him what he needed to learn. May his richest experiences be ones you curated and planned, not just random, traumatic events that lead to brokenness.

NOW THAT YOU'VE PREPARED your heart for that day, now that you've begun to think through the answers to those four questions, it's time to begin preparing the path. It's time to come up with your own vision as a father for what you want to impart to your son so that on the day he leaves your house, on that day the moving truck pulls up along the sidewalk, or on that day he picks up a suitcase in each hand, he will look at you and say, "Thank you, Dad. I am who I am because of you. Thank you, Dad. I know what I know because of you. Thank you, Dad. I can do what I can do because of you. Thank you, Dad, for the experiences you gave me."

QUESTIONS *to* Think About

☞ What are two or three of the top lessons you learned from your dad when you were growing up?

☞ Did you feel adequately prepared for the realities of life when you left home? Why or why not?

INTENTIONALSTEPS

This is one of the more involved intentional steps in the entire book, so take your time and work through each of the exercises below.

Exercise #1: Preparing for That Day

Answer the four important questions to think through before your son leaves home:

What do you want your son to know?
Who do you want him to be?
What do you want him to be able to do?
What experiences do you want him to have?

Know	Be	Do	Experience

Give it a lot of thought. Take your time. Dream big. You're only going to get one shot at this! Put some deep time into thinking through these questions before you move on to the next exercise.

Maybe a way to personalize this based on your own son is to imagine him saying:

> "Thank you, Dad, that I *am* _____ because of you."
>
> "Thank you, Dad, that I *know about* _____ because of you."
>
> "Thank you, Dad, that I *can* _____ because of you."
>
> "Thank you, Dad, that I got to *experience* _____ because of you."

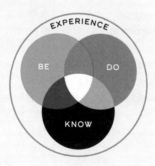

Exercise #2: Create an Asset Map

The next exercise in preparing yourself and your son is to create an asset map. You see, followers of Jesus have a tremendous advantage in developing young men because we're embedded in rich communities of other men and other families. We have a strong relational network we can leverage to help raise our sons in intentional ways.

For your asset map, I want you to begin by dreaming about the journey you're going to prepare for your son. What tools, what experiences, what people, what places, what trips can you put together in order to develop something extraordinary for him? What do you want to give him in order to help him get ready to go out into the world?

When I started creating an asset map, I realized I had way more resources at my disposal for my son's journey than I had imagined, and so much more than what I could have offered him on my own. I thought I had to come up with everything. I thought I had to do everything. I thought I had to pay for everything. But I'd forgotten I was surrounded by people who loved me and loved my son, and they were cheering us on and were more than happy to get involved.

I had access to some incredible experiences, significant people, extraordinary places, financial capital, and a lot of other things that, if I was strategic and planned well enough, would enable me to deliver something quite extraordinary for my son.

Assets available to me for this journey with my son:

Exercise #3: Form an Intentional Father Cohort

Consider getting a group of other dads together, perhaps friends from college or other men in your church, who have sons around the same age as yours—boys who are growing up together. Do this thing in community. When I started working through this with my own son, I found a small group of dads with sons Nate knew, and I sat down with them to present a vision for what I wanted to do for Nate.

"Let's do this for all our sons," I said. "Let's get this right."

We formed a cohort to walk together through the process. I felt tremendous support from these other dads, and Nate was blessed to have friends going through the same experiences.

So, start asking yourself, *Who could I do this intentional father journey with?* Sure, there are components, a lot of them, that will simply be one-on-one between you and your son, but knowing he's part of a larger tribe adds a lot of value and can be really helpful.

CHAPTER FOUR

Honoring Your Father

"Wounded?" was all I could manage. "Yes," said Pat. "And you're wounded in the same place. That's what fathers do if they don't heal their wounds. They wound their children in the same place."

CHERYL STRAYED

THE PRINCIPLE

We are called to deal with the brokenness of our past, understand the blessings we have inherited, and pass on a legacy of healing to our sons.

Y FATHER SPENT his defining years in a boarding school in India, enrolled there by his own father, who was a missionary. My grandfather was a very gifted teacher with a supernatural ministry, by all accounts a very godly man, but he was not a good father. He came from a generation that believed if you loved your family of origin, your spouse, or your children more than Jesus, you weren't worthy of him, so in order to minimize distractions, he dumped his kids in a boarding school, only seeing them a few times a year. As a result, my dad didn't have the tools he needed to make the transition from adolescence to adulthood.

No one gave my dad the sex talk. My grandfather didn't sit him down and teach him about life, how to navigate tough situations, what it meant to be a warrior, how to deal with money, or how to stand up for himself. Because my dad wasn't handed these tools, he wrestled with a lot of insecurities in many of those areas.

When he had me, he did his best, but he still struggled to impart the things I needed, because that skill of passing down, of raising up, was never modeled for him. I guess at some point we all have this realization about our fathers, that they didn't quite have the tools they needed to propel us into manhood.

In one of my favorite books, *The Bonfire of the Vanities*, the main character, a man named Sherman, is a bond trader living in the Upper East Side of Manhattan. At one point, the narrator explains Sherman's relationship with his father in this way:

> Sherman made a terrible discovery that men make about their fathers sooner or later, that the man before him was not an aging father, but a boy. A boy much like himself, a boy who grew up and had a child of his own and as best he could, out of a sense of duty and perhaps love, adopted a role called "being a father," so that his child would have something mythical and infinitely important: a protector, who would keep a lid on all the chaotic and catastrophic possibilities of life.[1]

Isn't that true? Our fathers were boys once, and very few of them were guided into manhood properly. And then our fathers were still boys when they had to take on the label of "father" to raise us, and many of them didn't have a clue what they were doing.

Have you ever thought of your father as a boy looking for love?

One of the profound things author Richard Rohr once said was, "If we do not transform our pain, we will most assuredly transmit it."[2] In other words, if we don't deal with our own baggage and our own hurt, if we don't walk into our own wounds and discover what is really happening there, we'll end up passing that pain on to someone else.

For fathers, this holds true: if we don't transform the pain we experienced as sons, we will pass that pain on to our own sons.

So many of us feel inadequate because of the fallout of what happened between us and our own fathers (or of their absence), which means we have to spend some dedicated time thinking through the role our fathers had in our lives.

Is it tough for you to think about your father? Maybe you're wishing he'd tried harder. Maybe you hear what other dads did for their sons at a young age, and it hurts because your father never did those kinds of things for you. Maybe Father's Day is the day you hate the most because there's a giant hole in your life that a father should have filled for you.

It's important to realize that all of us have complicated relationships with our fathers, whether because of what they did or what they didn't do. What we have to learn to do is actually begin to view them as men.

Psychologist Carl Jung taught that we truly become adults when we don't view our parents just through a chronological bias, but we see them as adults for who they are.[3] That's how we can begin to have compassionate understanding for them—they were young once too, and they're struggling through life, often with the same difficulties and insecurities that we have.

It's important we make peace with our fathers.

What I want to encourage you to do might not be easy for you. In fact, you might hear what I'm about to say and think, *There is no way I can do that. There is no way I am going to do that.*

My Father Figure

Four out of five U.S. dads (79%) say their biological father was their primary father figure during childhood. Another one in six reports a stepfather (9%), a grandfather (5%), or someone else (3%) filled that role, while 4 percent say they did not have a father figure.

Keep an open mind.

Here it is.

I want you to write a tribute letter to your father as a way of honoring him.

When I was preparing to go on this journey with my son, Nate, I realized I needed to have this kind of a moment with my own father, so I spent an entire evening thinking through my childhood and my relationship with my dad, and I wrote him a letter. I tried to list every single thing I remembered that he got right, and I opened the letter like this:

Hey, Dad, at this point in your life, now that I'm a man and raising my own son, you're probably wondering what I think of you. You're probably looking back over your role as a father with moments of pride and moments of regret. And I just wanted to let you know, here are some of the things you got right. Thank you for these things.

I wrote several pages of very specific things I remembered, letting him know what he had done, what those things did in me, and what I was grateful for. I closed it with a blessing of gratitude and said, "I want to honor you as a man."

My parents happened to be in New York at the time, and I gave the letter to my father before they got on the plane to fly back to Australia. When my parents got home, my mum called me.

"What did you write to your father?" she asked.

I was a little worried. "Did I offend him somehow?" I asked.

"No," she said. "Something profound happened in your father's heart. He sat on the plane weeping while he read your letter. He was so happy about it. Thank you for doing that for him."

I'd like to encourage you to do the same thing. Now, maybe your father was absent and you have to write a letter forgiving him. There has to be a moment when you draw a line in the sand and determine you aren't going to let the pain you experienced be transferred into the life of your own son. You have to decide to redeem what you've been through, and the best way to do that is to bless your father.

Several of my friends who were also taking their sons along this path told me they did this. One of them had an incredibly strained relationship with his father, and he said this was the hardest thing he ever had to do. But he took the letter and read it to his father in person, and it became a profound and powerful moment in their relationship.

You can do it.

Prepare your own heart.
Make peace with your father.

THE SECOND EXERCISE I'd like you to consider for this section comes from something I gleaned from Viktor Frankl, a psychologist who was imprisoned in Auschwitz during World War II. During his time there, he paid attention to those who made it through and those who couldn't overcome the terror, the mundane work, the lack of food and water, and the overwhelming sadness of their circumstances. He wrote a series of books after he survived the camps, the most famous of which is *Man's Search for Meaning*.

One of the exercises he writes about is called "mountains and valleys." It's very similar to the exercise I wrote about in my book *The Burden Is Light*, where I talk about creating a horizontal timeline where you list out your high moments and low moments. But I like Frankl's language more, this idea of mountains and valleys.

Reflect over your life. Ask yourself these questions:

*What are the most beautiful moments of my life, and what
    are the most broken moments of my life?*
What are the highs, and what are the lows?
What are the mountains, and what are the valleys?

The goal here is to begin to get a sense of your own story, have an awareness of the moments that have defined you, and remember the people who have shaped you. It's important to come to terms with your own story. Frankl said there's something powerful about stepping back, gaining an objective distance from your own story, and observing the things that have made you who you are.

Once you've listed these moments out, I want you to name them. Own the feelings that went with these experiences, and embrace how you responded, what you did. Think about how each moment has shaped you, whether it was good or bad, high or low, and try to understand how it has impacted the rest of your life.

Finally, ask yourself, *What can I learn from my mountains and valleys?*

This is the most important part, because once you can list the lessons, they become tangible things you can pass on to your son. Develop these lessons further as cautionary or celebratory tales you can share, walk your son through each experience, and reveal to him the contours of your heart. These are the things that have contributed to who you are, and they become the legacy you will pass on—they shape the values that are important to you and enable you to pass on transformation instead of pain.

So, that's your homework. Write a tribute letter to your father. If he's alive and it works for you, read it to him. If you can't read it to him, send it to him. If you need to forgive him, do it in person if you can, even if that's a difficult and painful thing. If you don't have a father or he's absent, write

Faith of My Father

Practicing Christian dads are more likely than the national average to say their own father prioritized faith (62% *very important*). However, a plurality of all U.S. fathers (44%) also say so.

HOW IMPORTANT WAS YOUR FATHER'S FAITH TO HIM?

% who had a father or father figure in childhood

● very important ● somewhat important ● somewhat unimportant
● not at all important ● I don't know

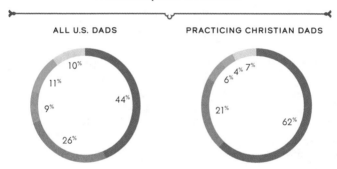

ALL U.S. DADS

10%
11%
9%
44%
26%

PRACTICING CHRISTIAN DADS

7%
4%
6%
21%
62%

n=542 U.S. fathers 18 and older who had a father or father figure during childhood, *n*=593 U.S. practicing Christian fathers who had a father or father figure during childhood, May 2020. Practicing Christians have attended a worship service within the past month and strongly agree that faith is very important in their lives.

it anyway and say things to him you wish you could say in person, all with the hope of releasing any pain and bitterness you have. Determine that you will have a clean heart when you finish, that instead of bringing pain into the life of your son, you're going to transform it into something new, something beneficial.

Then write out your mountains and valleys and draw them on a timeline you can use. Spend some time processing these, always looking for the thread you can pass on.

These exercises will take some time, but they are vital practices if you want to truly enter this journey with your son in a prepared and healthy space.

QUESTIONS *to* Think About

☞ Have you ever thought about the fact that your father was once a boy? How does that change the way you think about him now?

☞ Take some time to write a carefully crafted tribute letter to your father.

INTENTIONAL STEPS

Do the mountains and valleys exercise, writing out all the highs and lows of your life and the lessons you learned from each on the timeline below.

When you have completed the exercise, your timeline may look something like this:

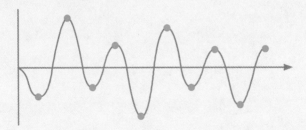

Each of these dots represents a moment, lesson, or highlight for you to examine. Here are some questions to help you extract meaning and understanding from these events:

What happened? *Name it.*

What did you feel? *Embrace it.*

How did you respond? *Own it.*

How did this shape you? *Understand it.*

What did you learn? *Extract it.*

How can you grow from this? *Use it.*

PART 3

...

INITIATION

Fathers Acknowledge Their Fears and Feelings

Half of today's dads (48%) say they felt *very prepared* to become a father—which means the other half didn't. About one in seven (12%) says they were *not prepared*, period. So wherever you land on the question of preparation, you're in good company.

HOW PREPARED DID YOU FEEL TO BE A FATHER?

● very ● somewhat ● not

12%

48%

40%

There's hope: For many Christian dads, *becoming* a father is transformative, even down to their core identity. In a study of men's self-perceptions and well-being, fewer than one in six Christian men who don't have kids (15%) told Barna they consider becoming a father central to their identity—but nearly six in ten of those who have a child (57%) say fatherhood is at the core of who they are. However prepared they felt before the birth of their first child, becoming a dad is changing them into a father.

Fatherhood comes with a lot of emotional highs and lows. Here's how dads tell us they feel, at least some of the time, about being a father.

THE FEELINGS OF FATHERHOOD

● proud ● excited ● confident ● exhausted ○ afraid ● inadequate

OFTEN		SOMETIMES	
proud	72%		25%
excited	54%		40%
confident	50%		45%
exhausted	22%		46%
afraid	16%		42%
inadequate	13%		37%

Only about one in eight dads (12%) says they never feel afraid. Lucky them! Here are some of the rest, in their own words, describing the parenting fears that loom largest. Do any of these feel familiar? Larger words or phrases indicate themes highlighted by a greater percentage of fathers.

MY GREATEST FEAR ABOUT FATHERHOOD IS . . .

THAT I WON'T BE AS CLOSE TO MY SON AS HE GETS OLDER

JOB LOSS

DYING

MY CHILDREN HATING ME

not preparing them for life, adulthood

LOSING CONTROL OF MY ANGER

NOT LIVING UP TO THEIR EXPECTATIONS

failure, screwing up my kids, letting them down

SOCIETY, THE WORLD

THAT A MAN WILL MISTREAT MY DAUGHTER

losing my child to illness or injury

PANDEMIC

NOT BEING THERE TO PROTECT MY KIDS

not being able to take care of my family

MY SON IS AUTISTIC—I WORRY ABOUT HIS FUTURE

n=562 U.S. fathers 18 and older, May 2020.

CHAPTER FIVE

Ceremony

Across time and place, cultures have inherently understood that without clear markers on the journey to manhood, males have a difficult time making the transition and can drift along indefinitely. Thus, rites of passage were clearly delineated in nearly every culture as one of the community's most important rituals.

BRETT MCKAY

THE PRINCIPLE

Adolescent boys need to know they are being invited into a journey of growth and development out of childhood and into manhood. There needs to be a definitive break from normal life into liminal space where they can emerge and grow as men.

I AM OFTEN ASKED, "When did you start talking to your son about taking him on this path to manhood? How did you explain what you wanted to do? How did you even determine what age to begin? And, most importantly, how did you get him to do it?"

First off, I let Nate know it was coming. But I didn't tell him everything.

When he was around age ten or so, I started dropping hints. "Hey, man, when you turn thirteen, you're going to enter into a sacred and ancient rite of moving from adolescence into manhood. And I want to tell you, this is going to be hard. It's going to be scary. You're not going to know what to do. But we're going to walk through this together, and you're going to end up loving it."

I tried to create a sense of mystery, some kind of holy fear around what he was about to enter into. And I also tried to create a sense of anticipation, excitement around some of the things that were going to go down. I kept it all very vague, but I wanted him to know that something was on the horizon, and it was a big deal.

As we got closer, I started counting down with him.

"Hey, Nate, just a reminder, as soon as you turn thirteen, you're going to get baptized into a journey into manhood."

By the time we got close to his thirteenth birthday, every time I said something like that, he'd say, "I know, Dad. I know! I wish you'd tell me more!"

Now, I chose age thirteen because almost universally this is the age at which other cultures have realized something happens in the heart of a boy. Something happens in his body, in his mind, in his psychology, and in his sense of self. He can tell he's beginning a new journey—he might not understand it, and most of it is going to catch him off guard if he has to navigate it on his own, but he knows something's coming.

But the whole thing didn't kick off with me. It actually kicked off with his mother.

In my research of how young men have historically been initiated into manhood, one of the things I saw repeatedly was a defining moment between mother and son when she directed his energy and attention toward the community of men and the challenges associated with becoming a man, rather than just the comfort she could provide. Marking this moment is an important part of his development and understanding of his masculine identity. We don't really have language for this in society today, so I'm suggesting a "directional dinner," where a mother points her son toward this new vision of development and formation. Young men need to know that everyone in their life acknowledges and supports the difficult journey ahead.

I talked to my wife about this, and it took a little vision casting and explanation so she could understand and support it before she agreed to do it.

This is how it went.

First, my wife took Nate to his favorite restaurant, which just so happens to be Outback Steakhouse. I know, I know—it's a total cliché that an Australian's son would choose to go eat at Outback. It's not authentic at all. It's like an Italian saying their favorite restaurant is Olive Garden. I realize this. Don't judge me.

She drove him across the river to New Jersey to this place where you can walk along a beautiful path and see the whole New York City skyline. It's a stunning view, with the high-rises and the skyscrapers and the bridges.

"Nate," she told him, "I'm the one who is going to actually begin the process of you entering the path into manhood."

She then took him out to eat, and while they were together she shared some memories she felt were important between the two of them. She'd thought through her experience of parenting him up to that point, and she had prepared to share some key moments, places that indicated his character or personality. She then prayed a prayer of blessing over him, and a prayer of release.

And she told him the one thing I had asked her to tell him.

"Nate, I want to direct you to your father and the process of formation so that you can learn to become a man. This will be hard, and this will be painful. And though I will be supporting you, it's important that you press into this journey and don't try to return to easier things. I will point you back to your father and this new community of men to help you move forward."

I don't know how she got through that, but she did, somehow.

Mothers are always important in their son's development, and this doesn't stop when they become teenagers. If you are a single mother raising your son, trying to work through these exercises and forming your boy into a man of consequence, you obviously don't want to sever him from your influence.

It's not that my wife stopped interacting with Nate or influencing him at all, but this was a moment for her to emphasize my central role as his father for the next season of his life. Think about a young man in high school who joins the football team. Of course, he wants his mother to come to the games on Friday nights and cheer him on, but if he gets hurt on the field, does he want her to come flying out of the stands, race onto the turf, and comfort him, right there in the middle of the game?

Probably not.

That's what I wanted these years to be like for Nate—his mother would show up, cheer him on, and encourage him after the game, but there would be some areas of his life where he would have to learn to rely on the community of men. (Years later, Nate would tell me this dinner with his mother was one of the most personally helpful things we did.)

When the two of them arrived back home, she came straight to the room where I was.

"How'd it go?" I asked her.

She burst into tears. "That was horrible." But she knew the importance of it. I decided I'd better go talk to Nate, just to see how he was taking the whole thing.

"Hey, Nate. How'd it go with Mom?"

"Well, she took me to Outback and I loved it. And she gave me some presents, which I was thankful for, and she said some really kind things to me. But it was actually kind of weird."

"That's okay," I reassured him. "It should be weird, because it's never happened to you before. Do you remember what she said?"

"Yeah. She's handing me over to you to become a man."

"Are you ready?"

He said he was.

"Okay, then. We are going to initiate you into the community of men, and it starts tonight."

I HAD WORKED IT OUT with three other dads that we would do our boys' initiation ceremony together, at the beach, but the boys didn't know this. All I told them was, "You're going to go under water, and it's going to be cold, and it's going to hurt. Get ready."

We drove out to Coney Island. I have this trip on film, and it's extraordinary. You could see the excitement and fear and fascination building.

"Do you have any idea what's happening?" they asked each other.

"No. My dad just told me this is the start, and tonight is our initiation into our journey into manhood."

We parked at the beach near Coney Island and went out onto the shore and sat in a group. We began by giving the boys a vision of what it means to be a man, explaining to them the path of men through history. We discussed the concepts of discipleship and formation. We told them there was an ancient pathway that all men of nobility walked, but this path had been lost.

Until now.

We had rediscovered this path, and they were about to be initiated into it.

It was such a powerful moment, and they listened with eyes wide open. We charged them with their responsibilities and their obligations, and we laid out a vision of what was going to happen on this journey.

After that, we had them strip down and run into the ocean as a baptism into the journey—and it was cold, which was perfect. These four boys splashed around and screamed and shouted and laughed, and then they were on their way to becoming men. Just like that.

When they came out of the water, we told them, "It begins."

We laid hands on them as a community of men, blessed them, and prayed for them. And we tried to call out their destiny, to call them into something. We celebrated the fact that a new journey was beginning.

When we got back home, I gave Nate a series of gifts that would serve as icons he could carry with him his entire life. The first thing I gave him was an awesome bronze pen that weighed about a pound.

"Your words matter," I told him. "They have weight."

A Community of Fathers

The Intentional Father argues that an important feature of initiating a son into manhood is a community of men to receive him. But some dads need to work on building such a community. Fewer than half of U.S. fathers strongly agree that they have a close friend who is also fathering a son.*

"I HAVE A CLOSE FRIENDSHIP WITH AT LEAST ONE OTHER FATHER WHO HAS A SON AROUND THE SAME AGE AS MY SON."

● strongly agree   ● somewhat agree   ● somewhat disagree   ○ strongly disagree

ALL U.S. DADS WHO HAVE SONS

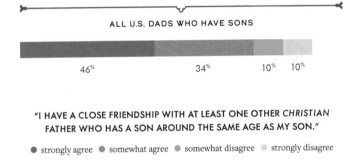

46%   34%   10%   10%

"I HAVE A CLOSE FRIENDSHIP WITH AT LEAST ONE OTHER *CHRISTIAN* FATHER WHO HAS A SON AROUND THE SAME AGE AS MY SON."

● strongly agree   ● somewhat agree   ● somewhat disagree   ○ strongly disagree

ALL PRACTICING CHRISTIAN DADS WHO HAVE SONS

56%   30%   9%   5%

n=451 U.S. fathers of sons, *n*=520 U.S. practicing Christian fathers of sons, May 2020. Practicing Christians have attended a worship service within the past month and strongly agree that faith is very important in their lives.
*Among practicing Christian fathers, just over half (56%) firmly assert that they have another friend who is at the same stage of fatherhood.

THE CONNECTION BETWEEN HAVING A CONFIDANT AND MEN'S WELL-BEING

% very satisfied among practicing Christian men

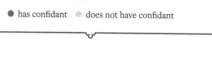

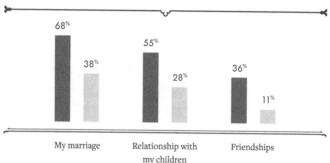

n=1,000 practicing Christian men 18 and older, October 8–21, 2019. Practicing Christians have attended a worship service within the past month and strongly agree that faith is very important in their lives. *Five Essentials to Engage Today's Men: Conversations Every Church Should Have about How Men Connect with Their Purpose, with Others & with Their Faith* (Ventura, CA: Barna Group, 2020).

I then gave him a beautiful leather journal, so that when we did our times together, he could write everything down. And, last but not least, I gave him something from the military: a beautiful, black footlocker.

Back in the day, when women were growing up, they had a hope chest their mothers would pack full of things so that when they got married, they could unpack the chest in their new home.

I wondered, *What are men carrying into their new home?*

I wanted Nate to have this footlocker in which he could store everything and anything he picked up along the journey we were about to embark on. Then, when he left home, he'd have all of these artifacts that would remind him of our journey together.

Finally, after I gave him these gifts, I prayed for him. I told him how proud I was of him. It was a powerful, moving night.

I've had other friends who have traveled this journey with their child, and some of them have done more than I did. Some of them have really knocked it out of the park. Some of them have done less. But all of them did some form of the severing dinner, and all of them marked the moment of moving into a new season with their son.

SOON AFTER THAT NIGHT, I laid out an overview for Nate of what we were about to embark on. I told him that every morning the two of us would spend time together before school, and that's when we would unpack the wisdom of the path together. And every week, the two of us would take one night together and this would be our version of man school—learning to be a man. These would be the times when I would pour into him. We would eat together, laugh together, talk together, and have fun, but we'd also dive deep. There would also be a monthly challenge during which he'd have to put into practice the things he was learning. And we'd take some key trips together that would stretch him.

That was it.

We were ready to begin.

We were about to take our first steps down an ancient, primal path.

QUESTIONS *to* Think About

☞ How do you think your son will respond to you creating an intentional, transformational path for him to journey along?

☞ What features of the way I set up the experience so far do you think would work with your son? What would you choose to do differently?

INTENTIONALSTEPS

Talk through the severing dinner steps with your wife and come up with a plan she's willing to carry out. Plan out the night and make it as meaningful as you can.

Brainstorm a powerful initiation, something your son will remember that will help him understand he is stepping out on a new journey. Take your time, make it meaningful, and go big.

Initiation Ceremony

Create an evening, day, or weekend to initiate your son into the Primal Path. Don't feel pressure to make this ceremony the highlight of your son's life, but don't wing it and underestimate its power. Try to include elements and relationships that will be meaningful to your son and will play a role in the path ahead.

When

What time and date will work? Is this connected to a birthday for your son?

Discuss what will work if you are doing this ceremony in a cohort to make space for a spread of birthdays. For example, rather than making the event connected to a date, you can make it after the last boy's birthday and say something like, "You have to be at least thirteen to do this." Don't get hung up on the technicality of a birthday if it doesn't work. Put the energy into the ceremony.

Possible dates for the ceremony:

Where

Place matters. Environments matter. Where is the best place for this ceremony to happen? Your house? Out in the woods? At a campsite after a hike? At the beach, at church, or on top of a building? On a special trip to a favorite or desired place? Make this a meaningful spot that your son will return to with joy.

Ideas for the location of the ceremony:

What

What elements will your initiation include? Prayers? Speeches? Laying on of hands? Gift giving? Words from other key men? The involvement of your father and other grandparents? Physical elements such as cutting hair or special clothes? Some sort of definitive moment such as running into the water, crossing a line, or facing a challenge?

Be creative, talk this through with others, and work hard to make it significant and enjoyable for your son. Make it something he will always remember.

One note on social media. I'm sure you will want to share this with the world, but I encourage you to keep some elements personal and private, something between the two of you that others don't know about. There is power in secrecy.

Ideas for the components of the ceremony:

Who

What men have played a significant role in your son's life? Who would you like to play a role in helping disciple your son in the future? Which friends and family would be significant for both of you?

Ideas for people to invite into the ceremony:

Artifacts

What memorable gifts will you give your son that will last well into his life? Examples include pens, leather journals, bags, articles of clothing, storage options for the things accrued in the coming years, Bibles, medallions, and morale patches. There are tons of options out there, so customize them for your son and his personal style.

Ideas for artifacts:

CHAPTER SIX

Home

No story has power, nor will it last, unless we feel in ourselves that it is true and true of us.

JOHN STEINBECK

THE PRINCIPLE

Until we know the story we are in, we will never know the character we are called to become. It is important that young men get a sense of a larger story and tradition, so they have some context for living well and break the delusion that the world revolves around them.

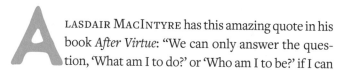

LASDAIR MACINTYRE has this amazing quote in his book *After Virtue*: "We can only answer the question, 'What am I to do?' or 'Who am I to be?' if I can answer the previous questions of what story or stories do I find myself a part of."[1] Young men today often grow up in a world where their story has no context. We often move away from our families and generational roots, and we have limited contact with our grandparents. As such, young men don't know the tradition or history or legacy they are stepping into. Context provides meaning and helps us know what to do with our lives.

I believe one of the great gifts that provides orientation and perspective for a self-focused teenager is to let him know your story—your family background, the place you grew up, and the moments that shaped you into the man and father you are today.

When I decided to do this, I realized I had to take Nate to Australia, where I grew up. Maybe a journey home for you doesn't require covering that much distance—maybe it means driving a few hours or visiting a neighboring state. But no matter how far it is, consider taking your son on a trip. Consider taking him home with you.

It's important that we bring our sons into our story.

I felt that Nate needed to understand the things that had shaped me and our family history. After all, if he was going to have some idea about what to carry forward with him, if he was going to understand me as a man, if he was going to understand the long arc of our family, I thought he needed to see what it was like where I grew up.

So, I designed a pilgrimage. I decided to show Nate where the major lessons of my life had taken place, from the mountains and valleys where I'd prayed to the places I'd learned my values. I wanted to show him the key moments, key places, and key people in my life.

What I loved was that he could tell from the beginning that this was a big deal—he had his journal out during the whole trip, taking notes, and was eager to be brought into the larger story of our family. He loved it when we showed up in Australia and he realized how *not* Australian he was. Everything he did felt other and strange, and he soon realized he was truly an American. This was all part of the trip, part of him experiencing for himself where he came from and how that compared to what he had become.

Some of you may know my story—I became a Christian the weekend I turned seventeen at a Pentecostal youth revival, just swept right into it. Prior to that, I had consciously thought that I wouldn't follow Jesus. Christianity seemed so boring and hypocritical to me, but then I met a group of the most passionate young people I had ever met. I was dating a girl and through her got swept into this youth group—and from there was compelled into the kingdom of God.

During that time of my life, I started reading as many biographies as I could about great Christian men, men whom I aspired to be like. And as I read about their lives, I realized that almost all of them got up at 4:00 a.m. and spent a couple of hours in prayer, first thing, before they did anything else with their day. As I realized this about my heroes, I decided I was going to be a 4:00 a.m. praying man.

There was a place I started going to in order to pray called Anstey's Hill. It was notorious when I was in high school. We would go camping up there, but rumor had it the Satanists used to go into those hills and sacrifice animals—the whole place was surrounded by these scary legends.

Time Well Spent, Part 1

Here's what U.S. dads say they're doing with their sons. Practicing Christians are similar to the national norm on most activities, except that two-thirds (64%) say they worship, discuss the Bible, or pray together with their son.

HOW DO YOU SPEND TIME WITH YOUR SON(S)?

Select all that you do together at least once a month.

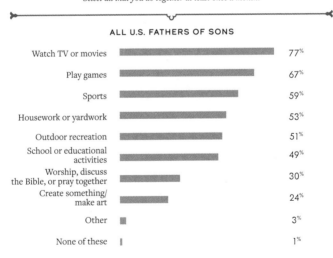

ALL U.S. FATHERS OF SONS

Watch TV or movies	77%
Play games	67%
Sports	59%
Housework or yardwork	53%
Outdoor recreation	51%
School or educational activities	49%
Worship, discuss the Bible, or pray together	30%
Create something/make art	24%
Other	3%
None of these	1%

n=451 U.S. fathers of sons, May 2020.

So, when I was seventeen, I started going up Anstey's Hill at 4:00 a.m. on my own, and it was terrifying. But I wanted to test my courage, to declare the kingdom of light as stronger than the kingdom of darkness. I went up this hill in the middle of the Australian bush and looked out over an incredible, panoramic view of the city.

"God," I prayed, "give me a vision for the world."

I had heard this story about Billy Graham, how when he saw the first images of the earth rising over the horizon of the moon, he hugged the television and started weeping. He saw the earth hanging there in space, hugged the TV, and said, "God, give me the world."

That story moved me so much I'd decided I would find high places, look out over whatever I could see, and say, "God, give me cities."

All of this to say, I took Nate to that very place, the exact spot on Anstey's Hill where I used to pray in the mornings.

"I asked God to bring me to America," I told Nate. "I used to pray in the mornings, and I asked him to open a door, to give me cities."

Nate knows how much I love to get up on top of a building in our own city and pray for New York, and I wanted to show him where that desire began.

"I was a teenager," I told him, "only a few years older than you, but I resolved in my heart that I would be a man of vision." And up there on Anstey's Hill, I laid hands on my son and prayed over him, that God would make him a man of vision, that God would lift his eyes beyond the confines of his generation and help him to see God's limitless possibilities.

That hill was one of our first stops. And it gave Nate a sense of vision.

After that, I took him back to the church where I became a Christian—I wanted to help him understand where my passion came from. At the time, it was called Paradise Assembly of God, but now it's Influencers Church. We parked in the lot and I talked him through everything that place meant to me.

"Look, Nate, here's the place where Uncle Darren and I used to come to pray in the mornings. Darren Whitehead, my best mate of over twenty-five years. This was where we would hang out. We drove around and prayed and saw God move."

I took Nate into the building where I became a Christian and sat on a pew, and again laid hands on him and prayed. "Father, pour the same Spirit and wisdom and revelation that you did into my life into my son."

I wanted him to see that this was where I first met Jesus, where everything changed for me, and where I received the vision to become a passionate man. We talked about dead religion versus passionate religion and why Jesus values first love. It was such a moving time, and Nate was able to understand the context of where I found and developed my faith.

AFTER THAT, I had the privilege of taking Nate to the butcher shop where I started working at age fourteen. I dropped out of high school at sixteen and worked there as an apprentice until I was twenty. This was a God-ordained moment—Nate had heard all of my butcher stories, and I have the scars on my arms to back them up.

Anyway, we pulled up to my old butcher shop, where I hadn't been in fifteen years, at least. We walked around, and I told him all the stories I remembered about working there, trying to give him a sense of this place where I learned how to work and developed my work ethic.

One of the butchers saw Nate and me hanging around, and I guess he got a little suspicious about what we might be up to. "Hey, can I help you at all, mate?" he asked.

"Oh, yeah. I'm sorry, I used to work here a long time ago. I did an apprenticeship as a butcher here."

"Really?" he asked. "Who was the boss back then?"

I told him the boss's name, and he smiled, "No way! He actually happens to be here right now!"

"No way!" I couldn't believe it.

"Do you remember where the offices are?" he asked.

"Of course," I replied. "I used to go get my paycheck there every week."

"Head on up there and see if he's in his office."

Nate and I did so, and what an amazing thing—my old boss was there! I was able to bring my son into the room and introduce him to the boss who had taught me so much about life. He had given me a vision of discipline, of how to work hard as a young man doing manual, physical labor.

My boss said something that made both Nate and me realize what a divine appointment that day was. "It's fascinating. We sold this business, and I am only in here for a few minutes today. We've sold the whole thing, including this building, and next week we'll be out of here. The fact that I got to meet your son, that you were here when you were, that's amazing."

My son got to meet this man who had shaped my life in so many ways, and I was able to talk to Nate about discipline.

THE FINAL PART of my story I wanted to convey to Nate had to do with the value of risk. I took Nate to the airport and handed him my two bags.

"You've seen my whole life here, Nate. You've seen the places that have had the biggest impact on me. I want you to imagine me packing all of it up into two bags, taking everything I knew, everyone I loved, every experience I had, and standing here in this airport, about to move to another country with only the vision in my heart of what God could do. I wanted to be a man of risk. If I hadn't done that, I wouldn't have met your mother. We would never have moved to New York. You would never have been born. Our church wouldn't exist. Everything you know and love about your life wouldn't exist."

I stopped for a moment. The people in the airport bustled around us. I could tell Nate was taking in the enormous weight of the decision I had made.

"That's the power of risk," I said. "Risk unleashes worlds of possibility and even paves the way for other people's destinies. Learn to step into it. Learn to embrace it."

What a powerful moment. I wanted him to see where I got my values. I wanted him to understand some of my key moments of pain and sadness.

Nate was young when we did this—it was toward the beginning of our journey together. You might be thinking, *Wow, your kid sounds supernatural. Was he really that intent and respectful? Did he really take this all in?*

Look, he was bored some of the time, just as any kid would be. He had his moments of wishing we would move on and of wondering *How long until we get there?* But the key to this step is to build in fun and wonder and joy, include things that arouse your young person's curiosity. Make it into a trip of a lifetime. You can do this if you include all facets of your story—not just events but also food and places and music and culture. All of it. Think big. There's a lot of good stuff for you to share.

For example, I took Nate surfing where I used to surf so that I could tell him stories about my old friends and the things we did when I was growing up. Some friends loaned us their car and a few boards, and we went out surfing at Middleton Beach in South Australia. I'll never forget it. When Nate stood up on a wave for the first time in his life, it was only for a few seconds, but the noises that came out of him were sounds I'd never heard him make before.

I paddled over to him. All around us the waves were crashing and swelling and the sky was a bright, bright blue. "Are you all right, man?" I asked when he surfaced.

Time Well Spent, Part 2

Here's what U.S. dads say they're doing with their daughters. Practicing Christians are similar to the national norm on most activities, except that two-thirds (65%) say they worship, discuss the Bible, or pray together with their daughter.

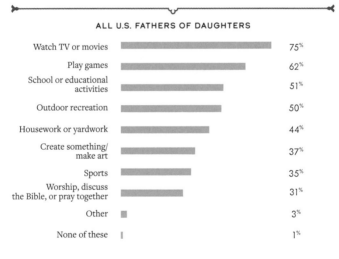

HOW DO YOU SPEND TIME WITH YOUR DAUGHTER(S)?

Select all that you do together at least once a month.

ALL U.S. FATHERS OF DAUGHTERS

Watch TV or movies	75%
Play games	62%
School or educational activities	51%
Outdoor recreation	50%
Housework or yardwork	44%
Create something/ make art	37%
Sports	35%
Worship, discuss the Bible, or pray together	31%
Other	3%
None of these	1%

n=413 U.S. fathers of daughters, May 2020.

He just grinned. "I've never made a list of the top ten moments in my life, but if I did, this would be number one."

Nate began to get a sense of what I did in my teenage years, and it helped him understand where I was coming from.

But there was more to our trip than just places and experiences. There were people too, important people whom he was able to spend time with. People like my father, his grandfather. In fact, I left Nate alone with him for two days.

"Will you just tell him what it means to be a Tyson man?" I asked my father. "Tell him about you and his great-grandfather. Tell him about some of our idiosyncrasies and some of our strengths, and whatever you learned when you were his age, and whatever you can remember about me when I was his age. Just pour into him."

So Nate spent two days with my dad, who poured solid gold into him. It helped Nate see me not just as his father but as a man and even as a teenager, someone who was his age once, someone who had his own father.

Finally, toward the end of the trip, my mum gathered a giant family reunion for a barbecue, and everyone introduced themselves to Nate. To be honest, it was a little strange—there were second cousins whom I'd never even met. But we took photos and laughed and got to know a few of them better, and Nate took away a sense that he's part of a larger tribe threading its way through history. He has some responsibilities, and he also owns a good inheritance that is his responsibility to usher forward, something to take care of.

One of the most amazing gifts we received was a book of family history from my cousin who has a PhD in history. He traced our family lineage back to the tenth century and compiled family mottoes, crests, and history all in one volume. We have gone over this several times together, and it has shaped our sense of shared history deeply.

The psychologists are right. Our families have way more of an impact on us than we're consciously aware of. How we are rooted, or not, into the world through our family relationships has a long-lasting impact. So, if we don't impart that legacy to our kids as they grow older, they are missing out. Without knowledge of that legacy, it's easy to become selfish and start to think the world's timeline begins and ends with us. We need a larger context to anchor us into the world.

Maybe you're wondering about the resources involved in making this kind of trip happen. Well, mine took months and months of planning and quite a bit of money, but I have zero regrets. It was so worth it, because it has become a reference point for both of us. It is a moment in time Nate can look back on and say, "That's where I come from. That's who I am."

QUESTIONS *to* Think About

☞ What are the key places and moments from my teenage years that I would want to share with my son so he understands me better?

☞ Who are the key people who've helped me become who I am?

☞ What are specific themes or words I'd like to impart on this trip?

INTENTIONALSTEPS

Create a genogram like the one following to help your son know your family legacy and history. Maybe there are things to be proud of; maybe there are cautionary tales.

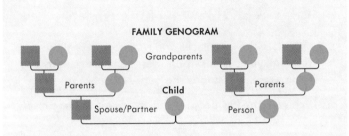

FAMILY GENOGRAM

Grandparents

Parents

Child

Spouse/Partner   Person

Exercise: Story Context Trip

When will you go?

Ideal dates for your work schedule

Ideal dates for your son's schedule

Ideal dates for your family's schedule

What extra help will you provide for your wife to make up for your absence during this trip?

Money for wife

Time alone for wife so she isn't overwhelmed

Chore helps for wife

Emotional support

Time alone for wife when you get back

Time for the two of you to debrief what happened on
the trip

How much time do you think it will take to do this trip
well? Your son will not appreciate being shuffled quickly
through the schedule like a tourist in your life. He is
young. Aim to process key memories and moments
with him and fill it with tons of fun that he will enjoy
and remember in between the heavier moments.

Where will you go? Which parts of your timeline
and story are important for your son to know and
understand?

Place 1 _____

Place 2 _____

Place 3 _____

Place 4 _____

What special things can you do that will make this trip
memorable for your son? What will create bonding moments that will last a lifetime?

Fun activity 1 ....

Fun activity 2 ....

Fun activity 3 ....

Fun activity 4 ....

What memorable ways can you show and impart your values to your son? What will help impress them upon him?

Value 1 ....

Value 2 ....

Value 3 ....

Value 4 ....

Who in your extended family would it be helpful for your son to spend time with to get an understanding of your family? Is there a family historian of sorts? Any family archives? Any old VHS tapes you can dig out to create context?

Family member 1 ....

Family member 2 ....

Family member 3 ....

Family member 4 ....

Remember, you want this trip to put your son's story in context and help him understand more about you. This extended time at the start of your journey can lay a powerful foundation for the rest of your years together. Don't skimp on it, cram it in somewhere, or wing it. You can tell your story well. Give that gift to your son.

What will make this a win for you? At the end of the trip, what needs to happen for you to think, *I did that right*? Go after that.

What will make this enjoyable for your son? At the end of the trip, what needs to happen for him to say, "Best trip ever"? Go after that.

CHAPTER SEVEN

Values

Here is the manliness of manhood, that a man has a good reason for what he does and has a will in doing it.

ALEXANDER MACLAREN

THE PRINCIPLE

Without values, a man is rudderless in a sea of relativity and compromise. With values, a man can navigate complexity and confusion with confidence and clarity. Infusing values—those of the family, those of manhood, and personal ones—is a great gift from a father to a son.

THERE WAS A TIME when we were planting a church in New York, but in order to save up money to afford living in that community, we moved to the woods. I was getting tired of all of the driving back and forth, all of the miles. One time when Nate was with me, I apologized for dragging him around during his teenage years.

"I'm sorry for making you drive this much, Nate. We've been going in and out of the city, and I hope you understand the mission behind why we're doing this."

I was going to keep explaining, but he cut me off. "It's okay, Dad. We're Tysons. We plant churches. This is what our family does."

My heart almost leapt out of my chest. I remember thinking, *He's discerned something here. He's figured out something key when it comes to the identity and values of our family.*

We're Tysons. We plant churches. This is what our family does.

From his perspective, church planting is what the Tyson family does. He's grown up around it. We've been involved in it. And he's sort of absorbed the idea that what comes with church planting is risk and sacrifice, paying the price, doing whatever it takes.

Naturally, I had to keep asking him questions.

"So, what else do you think the Tyson family is about? What does it mean to be a Tyson?"

We ended up having one of the most incredible conversations about our family. Of course, he also brought up a few things that were negative, things that were bleeding in from both sides of our family that we might be better off without, and we had an honest conversation about those things too.

But at the heart of that conversation was the idea of values. The things our family holds most dear.

What are your values? Have you ever really taken the time to clarify what you and your family are all about? We obsess over values in the workplace, our politics, and even the church, but few people do so with their families. I think it's very, very important to be consciously aware of and seeking to cultivate our values in our children.

Have you ever sat your kids down and said, "What makes us, us? What makes our family tick? Who are we?"

You might be surprised by their answers.

All of us at some level want to impart the values that matter to us into the lives of our kids. I want to really dig into three separate kinds: family values, personal values, and masculine values.

We'll start with *family values.*

Imparting your family values is crucial to this entire process. You can start by having an intentional conversation with your child about what they perceive as your highest family values, and that will give you a starting point. You'll see what's already in place as well as what you might need to work a little harder to instill or cultivate.

Next come *personal values.*

If you go back and look at the timeline you created in the mountains and valleys exercise, I think you'll find that your most important values have been formed and derived from those high and low times. It's after a mountaintop or

The Values Fathers Want to Pass On

Different people value different things. This goes for dads too. There is some level of consensus among U.S. fathers, however, around the values of respect and honesty, and, for practicing Christian dads, around faith, honesty, and respect. When it comes to fathers of sons versus fathers of daughters (see following page), the differences are not drastic.

WHAT ARE THE MOST IMPORTANT QUALITIES OR CHARACTERISTICS YOU WANT TO TEACH YOUR SON/ DAUGHTER ABOUT MANHOOD/BEING A WOMAN?

U.S. DADS' TOP 5 VALUES FOR SONS

1. Respect	54%
2. Honesty	54%
3. Kindness	32%
4. Faith	31%
5. Self-discipline	26%

PRACTICING CHRISTIAN DADS' TOP 5 VALUES FOR SONS

1. Faith	62%
2. Honesty	55%
3. Respect	47%
4. Kindness	33%
5. Compassion	25%

n=451 U.S. fathers of sons, n=520 U.S. practicing Christian fathers of sons, May 2020. Practicing Christians have attended a worship service within the past month and strongly agree that faith is very important in their lives.

U.S. DADS' TOP 5 VALUES FOR DAUGHTERS

1. Honesty		55%
2. Respect		48%
3. Kindness		36%
4. Faith		34%
5. Patience		28%

PRACTICING CHRISTIAN DADS' TOP 5 VALUES FOR DAUGHTERS

1. Faith		59%
2. Honesty		54%
3. Respect		47%
4. Kindness		39%
5. Compassion		33%

n=413 U.S. fathers of daughters, *n*=447 U.S. practicing Christian fathers of daughters, May 2020. Practicing Christians have attended a worship service within the past month and strongly agree that faith is very important in their lives.

valley experience that we walk away thinking these kinds of thoughts:

> *I care about this.*
> *I don't care about that.*
> *I'll get in a fight over this.*
> *I would get fired over that.*
> *I'm willing to go to war over that.*

Those are the kinds of judgments that become values in our lives, and so I want you to take some time to think through your personal values. What matters to you as an adult? What do you want your child to understand from your story?

I told you the four main values of my life in the last chapter: vision, passion, discipline, and risk. When I looked back over my own story, I realized that whenever I saw any of those four things in another man, whenever I saw the fruit of them on display, and whenever I was exposed to ideas connected to those values, my heart lit up. So, I determined in my early twenties that I was going to adopt those as my core life values.

Vision, passion, discipline, and risk. I wanted to pass these down to Nate, and I consciously worked to enable him to recognize them in other men.

Have you ever done a personal audit of your own values? Have you ever thought through the lessons you've learned?

If you don't impart your values to your son, the culture will impart its values to your son in their place. But you have a legacy to put into his life. You have a unique story of your own.

Finally, you need to impart *masculine values* to your son.

Philosopher Peter Kreeft argues that a key for renewal in any society is the recovery of the cardinal virtues.[1] He calls upon the Latin root for the word cardinal, meaning "hinge," to demonstrate that a hinge virtue is one from which all other virtues and values depend and flow. These values, according to Kreeft, are *wisdom*, *self-control*, *courage*, and *justice*. More than ever, we need to raise young men who have these values deep in their hearts. Imagine your son standing tall as a man with a life defined by wisdom, self-control, courage, and justice.

We need this change. Think about what frequently defines men in our mainstream society. The opposite of these values is often at play. Foolishness, excess, cowardice, and oppression.

Men sometimes use the strength they have to oppress other people; they draw on snippets and sound bites from random places as their source of philosophy, often without a historic or deep code of ethics. They are violent or passive, the two opposite sides of measured courage, and they are at times known by lack of restraint and given over to excess. Whether it be in the boardroom or the bedroom, men seem to have lost their way. Foolishness, excess, cowardice, and oppression are wreaking havoc and destroying men. But a recovery of the foundational values in men could heal society in a potent way. The Scriptures speak to these values, particularly as an exhortation to men.

We often think about Proverbs 31 as a description of the Proverbs 31 *woman*, but it actually begins by talking about *men*.

> Listen, my son! Listen, son of my womb! Listen, my
> son, the answer to my prayers!
> Do not spend your strength on women, your vigor
> on those who ruin kings.

It is not for kings, Lemuel—it is not for kings to
    drink wine, not for rulers to crave beer,
lest they drink and forget what has been decreed,
    and deprive all the oppressed of their rights.
Let beer be for those who are perishing, wine for
    those who are in anguish!
Let them drink and forget their poverty and
    remember their misery no more.
Speak up for those who cannot speak for
    themselves, for the rights of all who are destitute.
Speak up and judge fairly; defend the rights of the
    poor and needy.

vv. 2–9

This is an exhortation about what to do with male energy. Note the deep vision here about the kind of man needed to lead a society.

Wisdom. Listen, listen, a cry to observe and pay attention. Don't drift or coast through life.

Self-control. Don't spend your strength on women, don't drink too much. Don't let it numb you. Don't use your power or position for self-indulgence.

Courage. Speak up, speak up, don't be passive or quiet. Use what you have for others.

Justice. Care about the rights of the destitute, defend the poor and needy, and make sure proper judgement happens in the land.

Men who use their energy like this, courageous men, wise men, self-controlled men, just men—these kinds of men are the need of the hour. Foundational values in your son's life may lay the foundation for a renewed society.

I WANT TO BE CLEAR: imparting these values is not about fulfilling some sort of Western cultural stereotype of what a real man looks like. This has nothing to do with guns and trucks. The goal is to help young men fulfill their God given values of being conformed into the image of Jesus (Rom. 8:29).

And no one has embodied these values like Jesus. Think about his life.

Wisdom. Jesus gave us the Sermon on the Mount, a fresh vision of ethical love. He showed us the wonder of the kingdom through provocative parables and gave us truth that not only informs and inspires but also sets us free.

Self-Control. Jesus showed remarkable self-restraint when going to the cross, while being attacked by the religious leaders, as well as when the enemy tempted him directly.

Courage. Jesus boldly faced the cross when his disciples fled under pressure. He remained true to his mission when many turned away and laid down his life after wrestling with the consequences and cost of doing so.

Justice. Jesus advocated for the oppressed, created space for the outcast, and confronted hypocrisy in the systems of his day. Whether turning over tables, or welcoming tax collectors, he was working to make the world reflect the fair and just values of the kingdom of God.

Don't you want to raise up men with values like this, men like Jesus? Can you imagine what would happen with your son if he were inspired and equipped to live like this in these challenging times?

And so, have you codified your family values?

Have you codified your personal values?

Have you codified these foundational values?

In other words, have you thought through what they might be and made them tangible by writing them down somewhere and intentionally modeling them in your own life? And if you have gotten that far, how are you going to repeatedly model them? Hand them down? Demonstrate them? Call them out?

How will you mark these values in the life of your son and then reward him when you see him cultivating and growing in these areas?

In our home we established mottoes, and these helped us to constantly reinforce our values. For example, every day before Nate walked out the door to school, he would recite our own customized list of values. I recently visited him at college, and as he gave me a hug, they still flowed out of his mouth by heart.

I believe that if you get clarity on what you value, you're going to teach your son what's worth living for and show him a contrast of what it means to master the art of living. Resolve in your own heart that you will model and embody these values and pass on a legacy to the young men in your life.

QUESTIONS *to* Think About

☞ What are the principles, nonnegotiables, and values in my life? Do these values exist by default or design?

☞ How can I understand the right values, shape them, and pass them on to my son?

INTENTIONAL STEPS

Have a conversation with your child about what you each perceive to be the values of your family.

Review your mountains and valleys sheet and look at the lessons you've learned. What values have you absorbed from the highs and lows of your life?

Make a plan to impart these values into the life of your young person. How are you going to codify them? Embody them? Model them? Call them out? Identify their presence in your son's life? Celebrate the culture and fruit they bear?

The following values are especially unique to the ecosystem of men and are present in Christ. How will you
model and embody these values?

Wisdom ....

Self-Control ....

Courage ....

Justice ....

Exercise: The Values Audit

It may be helpful to take some larger sheets of paper
and brainstorm these sections.

Family Values

What do you regard as valuable as a family? Why?

How does this show up?

What values do you need to embrace to thrive and
function in your home?

How do you act when under stress? In joy? In
boredom?

This can be a great exercise to do with the whole
family and a good way to bring them into the Primal
Path story.

Personal Values

What matters to you?

What do you want to impart to your son?

What have you admired in others?

What have you learned about pain?

What have you learned about joy?

What have you learned about God?

What have you learned about yourself?

What aspirational values do you want to see developed in your son?

What values from your mountains and valleys exercise do you want to pass on to him?

PART 4

. . .

FORMATION

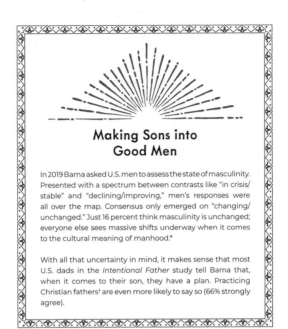

Making Sons into Good Men

In 2019 Barna asked U.S. men to assess the state of masculinity. Presented with a spectrum between contrasts like "in crisis/stable" and "declining/improving," men's responses were all over the map. Consensus only emerged on "changing/unchanged." Just 16 percent think masculinity is unchanged; everyone else sees massive shifts underway when it comes to the cultural meaning of manhood.*

With all that uncertainty in mind, it makes sense that most U.S. dads in the *Intentional Father* study tell Barna that, when it comes to their son, they have a plan. Practicing Christian fathers† are even more likely to say so (66% strongly agree).

I HAVE A PLAN FOR HOW TO GUIDE MY SON TO BECOME A MAN

% among those with sons

● strongly agree ● somewhat agree ● disagree

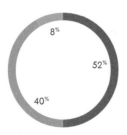

8%

52%

40%

n=451 U.S. fathers of sons, May 2020.
*Five Essentials to Engage Today's Men: Conversations Every Church Should Have about How Men Connect with Their Purpose, with Others & with Their Faith (Ventura, CA: Barna Group, 2020).
†Practicing Christians have attended a worship service within the past month and strongly agree that faith is very important in their lives.

What are they hoping the outcome will be? What do fathers want to teach their sons about what makes a man? Among practicing Christian dads, the top choice is *faith* (62%). Among all fathers of sons, *respect* and *honesty* top the list.

THE MOST IMPORTANT QUALITIES OF MANHOOD TO TEACH MY SON

% among those with sons; respondents could select up to five

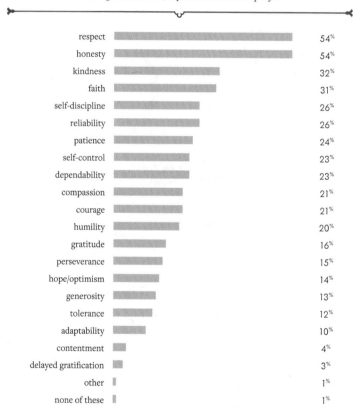

respect	54%
honesty	54%
kindness	32%
faith	31%
self-discipline	26%
reliability	26%
patience	24%
self-control	23%
dependability	23%
compassion	21%
courage	21%
humility	20%
gratitude	16%
perseverance	15%
hope/optimism	14%
generosity	13%
tolerance	12%
adaptability	10%
contentment	4%
delayed gratification	3%
other	1%
none of these	1%

n=451 U.S. fathers of sons, May 2020.

Forming Sons into Faithful Disciples

When it comes to practicing Christian fathers, the Lord's commission to make disciples is at least as challenging as the task of raising good men in today's culture. And being a Christian father means trying to do both! Three-quarters of these dads (76%) strongly agree they are focused on this mission, but they do it in many different ways.

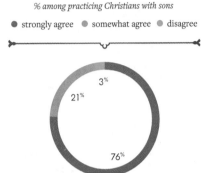

I AM FOCUSED ON TEACHING MY SON ABOUT HOW TO BE A CHRISTIAN MAN
% among practicing Christians with sons

● strongly agree ● somewhat agree ● disagree

3%
21%
76%

HERE'S HOW FATHERS ARE FORMING SONS

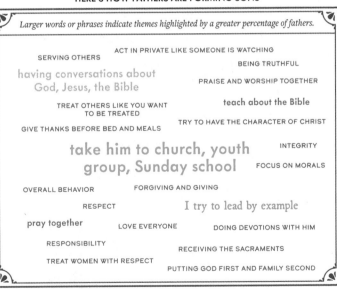

Larger words or phrases indicate themes highlighted by a greater percentage of fathers.

ACT IN PRIVATE LIKE SOMEONE IS WATCHING

SERVING OTHERS

BEING TRUTHFUL

having conversations about God, Jesus, the Bible

PRAISE AND WORSHIP TOGETHER

TREAT OTHERS LIKE YOU WANT TO BE TREATED

teach about the Bible

GIVE THANKS BEFORE BED AND MEALS

TRY TO HAVE THE CHARACTER OF CHRIST

take him to church, youth group, Sunday school

INTEGRITY

FOCUS ON MORALS

OVERALL BEHAVIOR

FORGIVING AND GIVING

RESPECT

I try to lead by example

pray together

LOVE EVERYONE

DOING DEVOTIONS WITH HIM

RESPONSIBILITY

RECEIVING THE SACRAMENTS

TREAT WOMEN WITH RESPECT

PUTTING GOD FIRST AND FAMILY SECOND

Christian discipleship is about much more than learning information about Jesus and the Bible. The greater challenge is learning to apply that knowledge to everyday life. Most practicing Christian dads are trying to guide their children to become wise in many different areas. Here's what fathers say they've been talking about with their sons.

I HAVE GIVEN MY SON GUIDANCE ON . . .

% among practicing Christians with sons; respondents could select all that apply

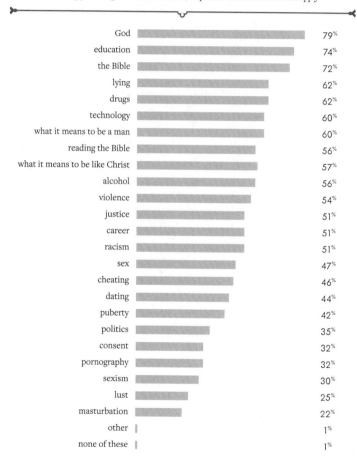

God	79%
education	74%
the Bible	72%
lying	62%
drugs	62%
technology	60%
what it means to be a man	60%
reading the Bible	56%
what it means to be like Christ	57%
alcohol	56%
violence	54%
justice	51%
career	51%
racism	51%
sex	47%
cheating	46%
dating	44%
puberty	42%
politics	35%
consent	32%
pornography	32%
sexism	30%
lust	25%
masturbation	22%
other	1%
none of these	1%

n=520 U.S. practicing Christian fathers of sons, May 2020. Practicing Christians have attended a worship service within the past month and strongly agree that faith is very important in their lives.

CHAPTER EIGHT

Five Shifts

Manhood is the defeat of childhood narcissism.
DAVID GILMORE

THE PRINCIPLE

To mark progress from adolescence into manhood, a boy needs to understand how boys act and think compared to men. He needs growth and direction and challenges to move along this continuum so he can see the progress he is making toward maturity.

I T'S NOW TIME for you to chart a course for your son from adolescence into adulthood. This is at the heart of being an intentional father.

Up until now, I've been taking you through doing a lot of event-type interactions with your son, and hopefully those have set a good foundation for both of you to build on. I hope they have given your son a deep sense that the journey has begun. But now we're getting into the daily grind, the long-term arc in the actual formation of his life.

Formation happens day by day; distortion happens day by day. We are either helping our sons move into adulthood or joining the culture's attempt to trap them in an extended adolescence.

There's a phrase my son would use when he saw older men who weren't leaning into their full potential: man-agers. They were like teenagers in a man's body, chronologically and biologically adult but still acting like adolescents.

This movement into adulthood won't happen by accident. We live in a culture that's confused about what it looks like to grow into the healthy life of a godly adult. A lot of masculine gifts are not valued in our modern world because so many men have taken those gifts and used them to abuse, overpower, and belittle others instead of serving others. This means it can be hard to step into our godly gifts as men with confidence.

The apostle Paul reminds us of the importance of this formation process in 1 Corinthians 13:11: "When I was a child, I talked like a child, I thought like a child, I reasoned like a child. When I became a man, I put the ways of childhood behind me." This is so important because it happens in the context of love. Remember 1 Corinthians 12 and 1 Corinthians 14? They're about spiritual gifts and spiritual power in the church, but right in the middle of discussing that power, Paul says, "Now let me show you a more excellent way" (see 1 Cor. 12:31).

This excellent way is the way of love. Until we manage to put childish speaking and thinking and reasoning behind us, we will not love well.

The five shifts I'm going to talk about are an important framework of how to do this.

So, HOW CAN WE HELP our kids enjoy adolescence while intentionally moving beyond it? One book written on this that I've read multiple times is *Adam's Return* by Richard Rohr. Rohr writes about five rules of manhood, five definitive things that have been poured into men in almost every other culture to help shape them and form them away from childish ways. These rules are:

1. Life is hard.
2. You are not important.
3. Your life is not about you.
4. You are not in control.
5. You are going to die.[1]

Sounds like wonderful news, right? Stick with me.

These rules are all true, no matter how hard they might sound, and almost all cultures have had ways of helping men understand these rules—except modern culture.

What does our culture tell us? Life should be easy, you're important, your life is about you, you should try to control everything, and you can live forever. And as a result, all of that emphasis on the self and self-fulfillment produces an extended adolescence, where men never grow up or reach their full redemptive potential.

Now, I have to admit, I first tried to impart the five rules to my son when he was very young . . . in the third grade, in fact. He gave a quote that was recorded in his elementary school as the quote of the week. With a huge smile, he said, "Life is hard, this is the first rule of manhood."

That was one of my prouder moments.

He didn't understand. No young man wants to hear the apparent bad news that these rules have to offer, but they do need to learn them. So, when Nate was a little older, instead of trying to directly impart these rules to him (again), I instead tried to facilitate contrast. I turned Rohr's five rules into five shifts.

Instead of saying, "Life is hard," I said, "It's a shift from ease to difficulty."

Instead of saying, "You're not important," I said, "Boys care about themselves, but men care about others."

Instead of saying, "Your life is not about you," I said, "You're part of the story, but you're not the whole story."

Instead of saying, "You're not in control," I said, "It's a
shift from control to surrender."

Instead of saying, "You're going to die," I said, "It's a
shift from the temporary to the eternal."

I began a period of time when I consciously wanted to show Nate that the life of a boy is a life of ease, a life of self in which we try to control everything, and a life spent living in the moment. But the beauty of being a man is that a man embraces difficulty, cares about others, is part of a greater story, is willing to surrender to a greater cause, and lives for the eternal, not the temporary.

Our core framework for walking through each of these shifts looked like this: during our morning meetings, I did a Bible teaching where I tried to point out whichever value we were discussing at the time. We read from Proverbs, the Gospels, the epistles, and the writings of Old Testament saints. We read biographies, and on a weekly basis we watched a movie that embodied the shift we were exploring. We had long discussions about what that journey looked like and what its challenges were, and toward the end of our exploration into each shift I designed an experience and challenge to show Nate the joys and possibilities that come with moving from one to the other. I tried to end each one with a deep sense of reward, something that left him marked with positive feelings about what he would be shifting into.

The State of Manhood Today

In a national study of U.S. men, Barna asked survey respondents to assess the state of masculinity in our culture today. Generally speaking, practicing Christians tend to be more pessimistic in their assessments than men overall.

WORDS THAT DESCRIBE THE STATE OF MASCULINITY TODAY

● all U.S. men ● practicing Christian men

MORE NEGATIVE
Perceptions of masculinity

MORE POSITIVE
Perceptions of masculinity

More Negative	all U.S. men	practicing Christian men	More Positive
Unhealthy	5% 16% 35% 27% 17%	10% 24% 30% 23% 14%	Healthy
Endangered	8% 23% 36% 21% 12%	14% 25% 33% 19% 9%	Thriving
Confused	8% 25% 32% 21% 13%	16% 31% 26% 16% 10%	Vibrant
In crisis	8% 21% 35% 22% 14%	13% 27% 30% 19% 11%	Stable
Changing	16% 39% 29% 25% 12%	21% 46% 25% 5% 2%	Unchanged
Threatened	7% 21% 32% 25% 14%	15% 29% 25% 20% 11%	Hopeful
Declining	7% 21% 30% 27% 14%	11% 30% 29% 19% 11%	Improving
Weak	5% 14% 36% 27% 18%	8% 24% 30% 23% 14%	Strong
Regressing	7% 20% 31% 28% 15%	13% 28% 28% 21% 11%	Progressing

n=593 U.S. men 18 and older, *n*=1,000 practicing Christian men 18 and older, October 8–21, 2019. Practicing Christians have attended a worship service within the past month and strongly agree that faith is very important in their lives. *Five Essentials to Engage Today's Men: Conversations Every Church Should Have about How Men Connect with Their Purpose, with Others & with Their Faith* (Ventura, CA: Barna Group, 2020).

It's important to understand that leading your young person through each of these shifts may take significant time. Be creative and customize it around your son—ease for him may look very different from how ease looked for Nate, and difficulty for your son might look different from difficulty for Nate. But if you take your time moving through them, and you're thorough and creative, they will eventually be able to rattle off the shifts, recognize the value in each one, and have a context about how each of these shifts will work through their lives.

And remember, these aren't just generic manhood shifts— these are the shifts that help our sons become more like Jesus Christ. Jesus left the ease of heaven to embrace the difficulty of earth and of the cross; Jesus humbled and emptied himself, and he lived for others, not just himself; Jesus moved into a life of obscurity for us; Jesus surrendered, not trying to remain in control of his situation; and Jesus lived for eternal rewards, not temporary reality.

Even though the ways I did this for Nate might look very different from the ways you do this for your kid, let me run through a few of the ways I tried to facilitate these shifts. Maybe they will help you generate some new ideas for your journey.

From ease to difficulty. Toward the end of our journey through this shift, I took Nate on the highest ropes course in the country. Truth be told, the heights were terrifying, especially for Nate, because he doesn't like heights. He really had to focus and work hard to overcome his fears, and the whole thing was amazing because he got up there and was able to go through the entire course. He actually found real joy in it, and it gave him a physical, tangible reminder that doing difficult things is rewarding.

Another activity we did—even though it sounds cliché, don't knock it—was watch the movie *Braveheart* together. Think about when you saw that movie for the first time, how new it was for you, and what an emotional impact it had. After we watched it, we had this fantastic conversation about William Wallace's desire for a life of ease and how he embraced difficulty. From there we went on to study the life of Sir Ernest Shackleton through reading the book *Endurance*, diving into the story of someone who did whatever was necessary to keep pushing and pushing, saw in the end what the fruit of difficulty can be, and accepted responsibility.

That was the journey from ease to difficulty, and while it was beautiful at times, it was also difficult—there were tears, and I pushed him, and sometimes Nate wept. It was hard. But, ultimately, he's so grateful that someone gave him a vision of embracing difficulty as a man, because there's a sense of respect—both for yourself and from others—when you rise up and embrace difficult things.

From self to others. I explained to Nate that he needed to realize life isn't just about him and he needed to learn to live for other people, so I had him join a serving team at our church. He chose the hardest team, the group who set up the church early Sunday morning and tore it down every Sunday night. And I did it with him to create some solidarity between us. The two of us would arrive at the high school where our church met to carry in the heavy speakers and all the other equipment. And let me tell you: there is no fanfare in this job, no glory. It's just setting the stage so others can enjoy an encounter with God that weekend. Nate stayed on that team and served there for a couple of years, and it was very life-giving for him.

From the whole story to part of the story. I wanted Nate to begin to realize he lived in the middle of Manhattan and had a very privileged life, and the story God was telling was way bigger than the streets he walked and the people he saw every day. I took him to different parts of the city and different parts of the world so he could be exposed to people who lived differently than he did, those with fewer resources, those who were underprivileged, those born into very dissimilar circumstances. I wanted him to realize life wasn't about him just getting everything he wanted, that he was actually a tiny little part of a very big story. This is a difficult lesson to teach teenagers, who often can't see beyond the boundaries of their own lives.

From control to surrender. Life is a challenge, and things are going to come our way we can't always control. Nate experienced this with the death of a pet. That might not sound like much to those of you who aren't attached to animals, but we lost two dogs in pretty close succession, and it was really hard on him. He had to learn what it's like to experience life as a challenge, and how to live through disappointment when things we can't control come our way. There are giant forces at work in life, and we're not able to make everything go our way. We're not God. We have to learn to surrender to him and his plan.

To add to this sense, I would push Nate into the woods to give him a feel for the wilderness, how he's not in control (although most of the time it might seem like he is). In the city, we can turn on a light whenever we need it, turn on water whenever we want it, and lock our doors to keep out the things we don't want, but out in nature it's easier to understand there are larger forces at work, forces we can't control, and we can start to imagine what surrendering looks like.

From the temporary to the eternal. "You are going to die." This might be the hardest one for a teenager to take to heart. I took Nate to a local Moravian cemetery, and I had him walk through the tombs for twenty minutes in silence and think about all the lives of the people who had gone before him. I wanted him to realize that those people had all lived their lives and now it was over for them.

When the twenty minutes were up, I asked him, "What did you see? What did you notice? You were walking over all of their dead, buried bodies. What did you learn about their lives from their tombstones?" It was a moving experience. We saw the tombstones of children who had died young and those of married couples who had died within weeks of each other.

I asked Nate if he noticed the common theme on all of the tombstones—there is the date of birth, the date of death, and the dash in between. "Your entire life is going to come down to that dash. That's your opportunity to shape eternity: eternal rewards, eternal fruit, eternal vision." I wanted him to see and somehow understand that his life would pass in the blink of an eye, that he needed to live for the eternal because the here and now would be gone so quickly.

This experience marked him so deeply that there are still times when he'll send me a text and at the end add #whats yourdash or #livingmydashwell. He caught the vision of a life bigger than himself, a life lived for the kingdom of God, a life lived with eternity in mind.

One of the bonuses of this particular exercise is that it will also affect your own heart as a father, a guardian, and a human being. I found myself inspired to move from ease into difficulty, to recognize the eternal in what I am doing, and to make all of these shifts more permanent in my own life. If you work hard on this, if you make it a meaningful time with your son, you'll be amazed at the fruit that results.

QUESTIONS *to* Think About

☞ When you look at the men around you, which shifts seem to be more natural than others? Which shifts are more challenging?

☞ Which of these shifts in thinking have you made as you entered adulthood? Are there any of these shifts you have not navigated well?

☞ Which do you expect will be the most challenging shifts for your son to make?

INTENTIONALSTEPS

Make a list of resources you'd like to use for each shift: Bible passages, biographies, movies, experiences, and anything else you can think of. Categorize them into the five different shifts. Plan to take at least a month or two on each shift.

What challenge or challenges will you use to help your child understand each shift and identify its rewards?

Use the following as a way to plan out each of the shifts to take your son through, from easy to difficult.

Scriptures to study:

Biographies to read:

Movies to watch:

Trips to take:

Places to visit:

People to talk to:

Cohort/solo events to attend:

Possible challenges to mark shifts:

Marking the moment and celebrating growth:

CHAPTER NINE

The Power of Preparing for Moments

I believe that what we become depends on what our fathers teach us at odd moments, when they aren't trying to teach us. We are formed by little scraps of wisdom.

UMBERTO ECO

THE PRINCIPLE

So much of our lives is defined by moments. Moments of wonder, moments of heartache, moments of accomplishment, moments of regret. An intentional father is aware of the power of moments and works hard in advance to create life-changing ones.

VERY OFTEN, when it comes to our own stories we are on a kind of autopilot. We rarely take the time to reflect on the events, people, and forces that have shaped and formed us. We can often see them in others but are sometimes blind to these things in our own lives. That's why it's essential, before we try to shape others, to understand the things that have shaped us. What has brought about the deepest joys and the most painful wounds in your life?

If we spend time reflecting, we can see that the joys and wounds in our lives often come from key moments when someone got it right . . . or got it horribly wrong. I can immediately think of two examples, two key moments in my own childhood with my father—one where he got it right and one where he didn't.

We'll start with the one he got wrong.

I hit puberty pretty early, and I was also really tall. I hit six feet at around age twelve or thirteen, and I was lanky, so I played basketball. I ended up devoting myself to the sport, practiced for hours and hours, and got really good.

I made it from our local league all the way up to the highest level of basketball I could play as a teenager in Australia, which was state basketball. I played for a team called SA Church, a really strong team. We even made it all the way to the finals and became state champions. It was the highlight of my early teen years, an extraordinary season of life.

There is one game in particular that comes to mind in which I was on fire.

I say that with all humility.

I was on fire. I felt like I couldn't miss a shot—it was just all coming together. And when you work so hard at something, when you spend hours and hours practicing free throws and jump shots and layups, and it all gels when it matters most, it's a beautiful thing.

I had so much momentum in that game, and the people in the stands were going nuts. I could hear my friends' parents cheering us on, even cheering me on specifically.

"Way to go, Jon! Nice shot, Jon Tyson!"

It was such a thrill.

I remember looking for my dad after a shot, just draining this beautiful three-pointer and turning toward the stands, looking for his approval. After all, he had brought me to the game. I knew he was there. But when I saw him, my heart sank.

My dad was reading a book.

My dad was there, but he wasn't present. He wasn't paying attention.

What's so important in that book? I thought. I remember asking myself that very question. *He's here to watch me. Why can't he watch the game?*

That moment ended up marking me in profound ways, one being that I resolved in my heart that if I had a son, I would be present. I would not be distracted.

But fast-forward a few decades, and I heard my son say, "Dad, can you get off Instagram, because I don't want you to document everything. I just want to live this time with you."

Ouch.

"You got it, man," I replied. "You got it."

The realization I wasn't living a life of presence with my son hit me so hard that I basically took several years off Instagram.

There's another moment in my mind, though, a moment my dad got right.

And in order to tell this story, I should remind you that I didn't become a Christian until I was almost seventeen, and before I was a Christian I didn't really act like one. Which makes sense, right?

This is the story of my first real fight, and it was a big one. I was fifteen years old and was dating a girl I really liked, but we broke up for one weekend. On that particular weekend, she ended up making out with another guy at a party, and on Monday the whole high school was talking about it.

I felt like I needed to confront the guy. He was about a year older than me and a lot bigger. His name was Clint. All of these thoughts swirled in my mind, the chief one being, *I think I'm going to have to fight Clint for my girlfriend's respect and for my integrity. I can't let him get away with that.*

It took on biblical proportions in my mind, this potential fight, and at some point during the day the classic words were said: "I'll see you after school."

I boarded the same public transportation bus as Clint. It was going to go down.

I was there without any of my friends, maybe not my smartest move, but I got on that bus knowing Clint was on it with all of his friends. They were all a year above me. The adrenaline started pumping—it was going to happen. I stood up and shouted at him.

"Come back here!" he replied from the back of the bus, surrounded by his buddies.

"Stuff you," I shouted back. "You come up here."

But after a bit more shouting, I thought, *Enough is enough*, and I made my way to the back of the bus. And I let loose. I started punching him in the face, and the bus turned a corner and I had him in a headlock, and his friends were all punching and kicking me. I refused to let go.

Then the bus wheezed to a stop, and I pulled myself away and got off. He had a massive black eye, and I was feeling sore but elated. His friends all spat on me out the window when I went past, and I ran all the way home.

It was a short journey from the bus stop to my house, and when I reached our driveway, I saw my dad working on something in the garage. My body was still on fire with adrenaline, my back was killing me where I had gotten punched, and bruises from being kicked were rising on my shins.

I looked at my dad and I said, "Dad, I just got in a fight."

He looked up at me. "Well, did you win?"

I grinned and said in an amazed voice, "I think I won. I think I won that one."

The amazing part was that he sensed what a pivotal moment this was for me, and he put his tools down.

"Tell me about it," he said, and after I described the whole thing to him, he told me a story about when he was in high school and there was a bully he had to fight.

It was this rare bonding moment. It was like my dad could sense that something big was happening and that I needed him to put down his tools and talk with me about it.

He got it right.

Making Time for Big Moments

In large measure, fathers of sons say they are intentional about marking important milestones in their young man's life. Exactly what events qualify as important—first shave? first date?—was not nailed down in the survey question, but most dads say they are making an effort to be there for the moments they feel are the big ones.

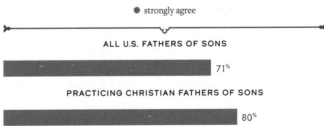

"I TAKE TIME TO CELEBRATE MY SON'S IMPORTANT MILESTONES WITH HIM."

● strongly agree

ALL U.S. FATHERS OF SONS

71%

PRACTICING CHRISTIAN FATHERS OF SONS

80%

n=452 U.S. fathers of sons, *n*=508 U.S. practicing Christian fathers of sons, May 2020. Practicing Christians have attended a worship service within the past month and strongly agree that faith is very important in their lives.

Now, I'm not advocating physical violence. That's not the point of the story. The point is that my dad got this moment right with his son, which brings me to another book I want to recommend you take a look at. It's called *The Power of Moments* by Chip Heath and Dan Heath.

It's an extraordinary book because it talks about how to build a moment in such a way that it touches you forever. And as a father, you're going to have a lot of these moments, times when you can get it right or get it wrong. One day, your son will likely sit down with his own kids, and he's going to talk with them about the key moments in his life when his dad got it right or when his dad missed it.

Children go through so much change during their teen years, and all through these years will be moments, opportunities for us to be present or to be absent, and we need to get them right. Moments mark us. They matter. And because of the way our brains work, the moments that take place in our late teens and early twenties are moments we remember more than other times of our lives. We give a disproportionate weight to them.

Here are some key moments I've experienced with my son, along with a few thoughts on how to prepare for them and get them right.

First cell phone. What are you going to do when your child gets their first phone? Maybe they already have one. Either way, now is the time to mark this moment and have a conversation about what apps they're going to put on their phone, how you're going to restrict access to porn, and how they should respond to bullying, sexting, and other inappropriate behavior. Now's also a good time to talk about the music they're going to listen to. The first cell phone is a moment for you to step up and have a lot of great conversations around all of these topics.

First exposure to pornography. How you handle your child's first exposure to porn will either set a pattern of godly repentance or a cycle of shame. It's possible to underreact, saying, "That's totally normal, don't worry about it." It's also possible to overreact and make them feel like it's the end of the world. But what if you said, "Hey, look, you know what? This is something all men wrestle with. How did you come into this?" We want our sons to learn to bring their sin to us so we can confess and process together. We don't want them hiding in shame. Turn their first exposure to porn into a moment, and have a conversation about it.

First shave. What a great opportunity to mark a moment! When I was talking with a friend about this, he actually wept. "My dad wasn't there to teach me how to shave," he said, and it was really a wound for him. You can get this right. You can say to your son, "Get in the car; we're going to the store to buy you a nice razor, some shaving cream, and some aftershave." Or you can take him to the barbershop to meet his new friend, the straight razor. Whatever the case, you can make this a really significant moment for him.

First girlfriend. This is the kind of moment when you can treat your son with real respect. It's so awkward at that age to like a girl, "fall in love," and try to figure out how to care for someone. Rather than mocking or making light of Nate's first girlfriend, I tried to be serious about it. I entered into this moment with him and didn't dismiss it as kids' stuff.

First breakup. This is a traumatic moment for your child—don't point out that they're young and that the love they felt wasn't actually real. Treat it with the soberness and seriousness with which they're experiencing it. Come alongside them. You might have to spend hours talking with them about it, but this is a moment you want to get right.

First exposure to drugs. Have you prepared yourself to talk through this with your child, either when they first see someone using drugs or if they try it for themselves? This is coming. The legalization of marijuana is happening all over the country, and there has been a normalization of drug use in our culture. Are you ready for this moment?

First exposure to the LGBTQ world. How you handle this topic with your child is vital. You're either going to show the mercy of Jesus or the condemnation of the Pharisees. I have had this conversation with Nate. We live in a gay neighborhood in Hell's Kitchen, New York City. I knew I wanted to display the mercy of Jesus. What's it going to be for you? How are you approaching this moment?

First exposure to death. When our kids encounter death, their illusion of immortality is shattered. How will you help them grieve and face their sorrow? How will you handle the questions they're bound to ask? You can give them space, you can engage their questions—have you thought through how you'll handle this moment?

First job. I remember telling Nate, "It's time for you to get a job, earn some money, and learn responsibility." So he decided to apply for a job at Chick-fil-A, and I helped him prepare for his interview. We studied together. I coached him through what the interview might look like. And after he got his first job, we celebrated; we went out and marked this moment. I made him read *Why Work?* by Dorothy L. Sayers, and we talked about the power of vocation. It was a beautiful moment that shaped him.

First exposure to racism. We live in a divided world. You know it and I know it, but there's something important about that first moment when your child recognizes it. Are you prepared to have that conversation? What do you do? And how do we call out the church when it gets this wrong? What does biblical justice look like?

First time with a driver's license. Driving a car and the independence that goes along with it could possibly be the most definitive moment in a teenager's life. They can go anywhere and do anything. Their autonomy and freedom are dramatic. So how will you help them be responsible? Teach them what to do if there is an accident? Maintain and care for the car?

Whimsical moments. These other moments I've mentioned can be prepared for; with enough discipline, you can be ready for them. You can execute a plan. It's like a martial art—you run through something enough times, and then when the real thing comes along, your reflexes kick in and you know exactly what to do.

But whimsical moments are different. Can you somehow prepare yourself, when an unexpected moment happens, to knock it out of the park?

One example of a whimsical moment for us was when Barack Obama was elected as president. This was a big moment in the history of the nation—we'd gone from being slaveholders to having an African American in the White House. That's powerful. Nate was asleep when the election results came in, so I woke him up and said, "Nate, regardless of whatever political view you have later in life, tonight is a historic moment." At the time, we didn't live that far from Harlem, and I wanted him to hear the streets filled with people weeping and celebrating. I wanted that to shape his understanding of progress and justice in the nation.

Now, when you hit these breakthrough moments, some of them are going to overwhelm you. Some will feel like they've come out of nowhere to punch you right in the gut, and you're left reeling. You're not going to get all of them right. No one can. But if you make an effort ahead of time to prepare for these moments, your child will notice. They will feel it.

There's a line from *The Power of Moments* that resonated with me so much, and it's this: "Beware the soul-sucking voice of reasonableness."[1] These moments I'm talking about have the power to change our lives forever, but they won't be as powerful if we try to be just reasonable. We have to be unreasonable in the way we mark these moments.

What if your son told you he'd never had a Philly cheesesteak? Now, there are a few different ways you could mark this moment. You could jump in the car and head to the mall, have a perfectly nice afternoon with your teenager, and treat him to his first cheesesteak. Maybe you could even see a movie afterward, and by the time you come home, you'll feel good about things.

That's a solid game. That's strong. Great.

But you want to talk about the power of a moment? You want to talk about the power of being unreasonable? What if you said to your son, "Let's go get a Philly cheesesteak. In Philadelphia." And you realize there is a place that sells $100 Philly cheesesteaks, so you get your suits on. You drive to Philly. You get the expensive cheesesteak. You spend the night in a hotel. You go see a Phillies game together. And then you drive home.

Twenty years later, which moment do you think your son will remember?

Jon, that's not possible. We can't afford that. It's not practical.

Beware the soul-sucking voice of reasonableness.

Your children will leave your house, and these moments are going to happen. You have the power to shape them. Be intentional, not reasonable. You get one shot.

QUESTIONS *to* Think About

☞ What moments did your parents get right? What moments did they get wrong? How have these shaped you?

☞ Are there moments I didn't mention that you want to make sure you mark for your child?

INTENTIONALSTEPS

Develop a list and design experiences to help mark these moments in the life of your son.

Is there a whimsical moment you can go ahead and do today?

Master Moments List for Your Son

What is the moment? Why does it matter? How will you mark it? Included below are some example moments you may want to think through and plan for your son.

Getting a phone   First shave

Wet dream   First girlfriend

First exposure to porn   First breakup

Exposure to drugs

Gender, gay rights, human sexuality

First fight

First death

First loss in something that matters to him

First job

First paycheck

Racism and privilege

Getting his license and first car

Prom

Graduation

Baptism

Bullying

Lying to you, your wife, or other authority figures

Doubts about faith

Record other key moments you think may be important in the formation of your son. What specific things can you take into account regarding his personality, preferences, and desires?

CHAPTER TEN

Being Good at Being a Man

If there is no struggle, there is no progress.

FREDERICK DOUGLASS

THE PRINCIPLE

Young men today don't aspire to a moralistic vision of generic goodness. They want a deep understanding of what a man actually is and how to be good at that. They want the vision and skill to master the art of manhood. In this framework, confidence comes through competence. We must learn to transfer the tangible skills and the key elements of manhood to our sons.

I HOPE YOU'RE STILL WITH ME. Planning out how to lead your kid through the five shifts can take some time, and hopefully it hasn't been overwhelming. This journey is hard work, and in most cases this is at least partly because no one ever did this for you, so it's difficult to know where to begin and what to do. As you are probably seeing by now, this is about your own formation as much as it is about the formation of the young person with whom you're walking through it. But if you do it, if you commit to the process, courage and confidence will begin to rise in your own spirit too.

In the interest of full disclosure, I have to warn you that something will happen to your son as he gets older that will complicate this journey you're on. It's called the teenage years. He'll start getting interested in girls, he'll start joining sports teams or other groups that take up a ton of his time, and he'll have more academic pressure as he moves into high school.

Teen life gets more complicated, and as it does, keeping your teen (and yourself) on track becomes more and more difficult.

After we did the five shifts, Nate started to lose interest in the stuff we were doing. I think the whole process started to feel a little clichéd to him, and I was running out of momentum because I'd been doing this thing with him for a few years and was struggling to keep it all planned out ahead of time. I was scrambling to pull it off. And so, we hit a wall.

I remember a specific moment Nate came to me and said, "Dad, why do I have to get up in the morning and do this stuff? Why, whenever we're spending time together, does there have to be a lesson? Why can't I just be a teenager like all of my friends?"

The first thought that raced into my head was, *I know your friends, and I have spent time with your friends, and I don't want to be judgmental, but* . . .

But I didn't say that out loud. It was one of those early mornings, the same kind of early morning we had been spending together for quite a while by then. I took a deep breath.

"You know what?" I said. "That's a great question. Let me think about it for a minute, and I'll tell you why."

My desire in that moment was not to give him a trite convincing answer or say something that would talk him into staying on track with me—I really wanted to get to the heart of his lack of motivation to keep going. And what came to my mind was the secular critiques leveled against the Christian men's movement.

The pushback generally levels that the reason Christian men's movements are largely cliché or ineffective is that they are usually all about being a good man. A good man—what comes to mind when you think of a that? Often it's someone in baggy khaki pants and unpolished shoes with a tucked-in polo shirt that doesn't fit properly. He spends his life wrestling with insecurities and trying not to do bad things.

By the way, if you wear baggy khaki pants, I love you.

What I'm trying to say is that our common definition of what makes up a good man is actually not that inspiring. Christianity hasn't done a good job of raising up men we can look at and think, *Now, that's a good man. That's what a good man is, and it's amazing.* Few of us, when thinking of a good man, think of the wildness or passion of Jesus Christ—and if we do think of Jesus, it's because we've reduced him to an overwhelmed suburban dad who doesn't have time in his schedule and is always flushed and struggling rather than living with freedom, power, and authority.

I realized that this was true of how I pictured a Christian man. And, even more importantly, I had this breakthrough that Nate thought I was trying to make him into something along those lines—a good Christian, a good man.

"Nate, why are we doing all of this stuff together?" I asked him at last. This became a question I asked him every morning after that.

"Because you want me to be a good man," he replied. Those were literally the words that came out of his mouth.

"You're wrong," I said.

"What?"

"You're wrong. I don't want you to be a good man."

"You don't?"

"What do you think a good man is?" I asked him.

And, I kid you not, he went on to list many of the traits that secular authors critique about Christian men. "Well, it's someone who doesn't look at porn. Someone who tries to do the right thing," he said.

I tried to summon my inner John Keating, Robin Williams's character from the movie *Dead Poets Society*.

"That sounds boring. Is that what you think I'm like?"

"No, no, no," he insisted. "You've got passion in your heart. You've got a cause. All of that stuff."

"Then why am I going to try to make you boring?"

"I don't know. You tell me. You're the one running the show."

"Nate, I'm not trying to make you into a good man. I want you to be good at being a man. That is fundamentally different. I want you to have confidence in all areas of your life, where you can walk into any situation and you can say in your heart, 'I can do this.'"

We might have a lot of good men in our culture, but most are not good at being men. Hopefully, we all grow over time through skill acquisition.

What It Means to Be a Man

Half of U.S. dads who have a son (53%) say they've given their boy guidance on "what it means to be a man." Among practicing Christians, three out of five (60%) say they've offered guidance in this area. Going a step further into the realm of faith, three out of four practicing Christian fathers (76%) strongly agree they are "focused on teaching my son about how to be a Christian man."

When I was fourteen, I started the first job I ever had. I was given the task of sweeping up the front of a butcher shop, which was situated along one of the main roads in my suburb. I was told to sweep, but the interesting thing was, I didn't really know how. I mean, if you've never swept before, how awkward does that feel?

My boss came out and stood there quietly on the other side of the room, and he put his finger up, making the number one sign. He just held it there while I swept, and eventually my curiosity got the better of me. I walked over to him.

"Excuse me, sir. I see you're holding up your finger. What are you doing?"

"You are working so slowly that I had to put my finger up to see if you were even moving at all."

I got the point pretty quickly. "Well, sir, if you'll show me how to sweep, I will sweep very well."

He took the broom and showed me how to work faster, and this began the process of older men coming around me and raising me over time. I remember that when I became an apprentice butcher, I began learning bit by bit. It all started by watching, and I wanted to be good at being a butcher. I didn't just want to be a good butcher. So all along the way these men gave me little bits of skill and feedback and insight, taking me from a place of "I want to do this but I can't," to "I can do this and actually I'm very good at it."

It was a beautiful thing that happened over time: learning skills in sequence, taking on new roles, and handling new tools during that four-year period. At the beginning, I could barely hold a knife without cutting myself, and at the end, I could break down any animal you threw in front of me and turn it into the best barbecue you've ever had.

I went from being an observer to being someone with competence. Someone with skill.

This is key. This is what men need. All of us need actual discipleship and development, specific advice and skills and ways of living in the world that help us learn how to be good at being men.

One of the things I used to say to Nate all of the time that was not helpful in the least—and I think a lot of dads do this—came in the form of pep talks. I used to be especially guilty of this at sporting events.

"You can do it, you can do it. C'mon, get out there," I would shout from the stands.

One day, Nate came back to where I was sitting, nearly in tears, and said, "Dad, I can't do it. Your pep talks aren't working. I don't know what to do."

What a breakthrough moment.

Far too often, this is how we interact with the next generation of young people. We're on the sidelines telling them to keep going, telling them they can do it, and they're out there in the middle of their crazy lives thinking, *I don't know what to do. I don't know how to keep going.* This is why I decided to shift my vision of Christian manhood away from someone who is generically good at something to someone who is skillful at living well as a man.

And this changed everything for me and Nate, to the point where he said, "Dad, I'll wake myself up every morning for this. I want to be good at being a man."

Somewhere in this conversation is the beginning of role or archetype. What does it mean to be good at being a man? A man is good at understanding and interacting with women. We should learn about that. A man is good at understanding the role and place of money in his life. We should learn about that. A man has self-control. We should learn about that. A man knows how to be a brother to other men. We should learn about that.

My son began to get a vision of actually living skillfully as a man because—and here's the real breakthrough—confidence comes from competence.

That's one of the main challenges men face these days, at least as I see it: because men have such a low level of competence in any measurable framework, we have men who lack any sort of confidence. A lack of confidence manifests itself in . . . well, just look around at the way men behave in our culture. Angry. Fearful. Lashing out. Apathetic. Self-centered. The list goes on and on.

Confidence comes from competence.

Once I realized this, it shaped the way I interacted with my son through this whole process. In fact, I borrowed a framework from Dave Ferguson's book *Exponential*.[1] This is how it goes. I'll tell you about it first, and then I'll show you an example of how I lived this out with Nate.

Are you ready? Here is the process for discipling your son:

I do, you watch, we talk.

I do, you help, we talk.

You do, I help, we talk.

You do, I watch, we talk.

You do, someone else watches.

This changes everything.

One area Nate struggled in was hosting conversations with his friends. It can be hard to figure out conversational threads in groups of young people—they're jumping all over each other, they're on their phones, they're interrupting and laughing and talking in fragments. Nate constantly found himself talking over other kids in order to get his point across, or other kids were talking over him.

"Dad, can you help me with this? I want to be able to host a conversation. I want to be able to talk well with my friends."

"Okay," I said. "I can help you figure that out."

As we arrived at our next meeting with our cohort of other fathers and sons who were also going through this material, I said to Nate, "Okay. What we're going to do is this: I'm going to introduce a conversation and I'm going to guide that conversation toward a conclusion." I picked football, and I focused on one of the New York teams that was doing quite well at the time. I have to admit, this was a challenging topic for me because I didn't grow up in America.

"I want you to watch me guide the conversation," I told Nate. "Afterward, we're going to talk and I want you to tell me a few things you learned."

He sat next to me at the dinner table, and when I started talking about football I put my hand on his leg and squeezed it. Sure enough, it went really, really well. Nate and I had actually been reading Dale Carnegie's classic book *How to Win Friends and Influence People*, which includes many practical tools for communicating well. I used those tools in the conversation, and they worked.

On our taxi ride home, Nate was excited. "I can't believe that, Dad. You literally did what you said, and what the book taught actually worked."

I smiled. "Isn't that amazing? Can you see now that leading a conversation isn't a mystery and it's not all charisma? It's literally just competence and having the skills and learning how."

"This is incredible," he said.

"At our next meeting, we'll do it again, but I'm not going to lead as strongly, and I want you to help. I'll throw a topic out there, and then I want you to be the guardrails when the topic goes off track. I want you to be the one to say something that brings it back to the core topic. Agreed?"

He was totally on board at this point.

At our next dinner, I brought up a different point, and Nate helped to guide the group through the conversation. Afterward, I asked him how it went.

"It was amazing! I could see that one of my friends kept going off track, so I tried to get behind his thoughts so I could bring us back to the topic we had agreed to talk about. I learned so much."

"At the next dinner," I said, "you're going to do it. You're going to introduce the topic, and then I'm going to help you."

I have to admit—he was terrified. So we worked on it a bit, he picked a topic, and then at the next dinner, he brought it up. I provided some very strong guardrails to the conversation.

"Hey, Nate, actually . . ."

"Everyone, listen for a second. What did you say, Nate? Say that again."

Afterward, we talked about how it felt to lead a conversation, how he thought it went, and what he'd try to work on the next time.

At the next opportunity, he led the conversation and I just sat back and listened. I let him meander his way through it, and I realized that over time he had gone from someone who didn't have a clue how to host a conversation, someone who felt overwhelmed and ill-equipped, to someone who had confidence because the skills had been imparted to him and he had been led into the situation little by little, over time.

THINK ABOUT THIS PROCESS as you begin to move toward helping your son live into the roles of manhood. We'll get into those roles in the next chapter, but in the meantime, I really want you to think through the process:

I do, you watch, we talk.

I do, you help, we talk.

You do, I help, we talk.

You do, I watch, we talk.

You do, someone else watches.

Start to use this process when opportunities come up to teach your son something. This can work when it comes to changing a tire or writing a check or starting a blog. Anything.

And keep in mind, always, that your son doesn't want to be a good man, because who even knows what that means? Your son aches to be good at being a man, just like you do, and if you can begin to help him gain competency in manhood, he'll move through his adolescence and into adulthood full of confidence and life.

QUESTIONS *to* Think About

☞ What comes to mind when you think about a good man?

☞ What comes to mind when you think about being good at being a man?

☞ How can you cast a vision of being strong, being courageous, and living from a full heart to your son? What needs to change in you for this to happen?

INTENTIONALSTEPS

What are some things in which your son has natural interest and you could help him achieve competency? Make a list, and then be prepared to add to that list in the next chapter.

Make a list of the skills you wish someone had taught you when you were approaching adulthood.

CHAPTER ELEVEN

Roles to Master

We don't need to reinvent manliness. We only need to will ourselves to wake up from the bad dream of the last few generations and reclaim it, in order to extend and enrich that tradition under the formidable demands of the present.

WALLER R. NEWELL

THE PRINCIPLE

In order for your son to be good at being a man, he needs to understand and grow in the key roles of manhood. Learning and growing in knowledge, skill, and character in those areas will produce confidence as he moves out into the world.

MAGINE A FARMER walked down a backcountry road and saw another farmer repairing a fence. His young sons were helping him.

"Why are you letting your sons help you?" the first farmer asked. "It's going to take five times as long. You should just do it yourself."

"Oh, but you've made a mistake," the second farmer said. "You think I'm repairing a fence. I'm not. I'm raising my sons."

The first time I heard this parable, it filled my heart with a vision of the role I was actually playing by inviting my son into my life. Yes, some of these things might take a lot longer than we'd like. Raising a son is real work, but we have to get this right, because if we don't teach our sons, the world will. If we don't teach our sons about women, pornography will. If we don't teach our sons about friendship, they'll live a life of loneliness. If we don't teach our sons about leadership, they'll be followers all of their lives.

Being a father is not about efficiency; it's about discipleship. Being a father is not about time management; it's about heart development.

IN THIS CHAPTER we will cover the six roles a man needs to master to be good at being a man. This section of the journey may be intimidating to teach our sons because we don't know so many of the answers ourselves. A skillful and holistic vision of these roles may never have been imparted to us. The gift of this part of the journey, however, is that you can use it as a time of self-discovery, a time to fill in the gaps of your own development and formation.

We have talked about imparting a vision of being good at

being a man, and we've gone over a good method for handing down the skills, so now we're going to talk about six roles men need to learn to master. These roles have historically existed in all our societies, and they're commonly referred to as *archetypes*. Now, what we need to avoid is mistaking an archetype for a stereotype. It's easy for that to happen, but if we stick to the underlying truths, they will serve us well.

Role #1: Disciple

Not only is there a gaping father wound in our culture, but there is also a discipleship wound in our churches. If you were to go into a church and ask the congregation to put their hands up if they felt they had been properly discipled, you would see very few hands. If you followed that up by asking how many people would like to be discipled, to be deliberately led in a way that helps them to learn about life

Being a Christian Disciple

A majority of practicing Christian dads say they've given their son guidance on the following faith-related topics:

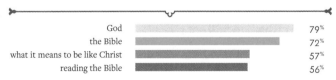

God	79%
the Bible	72%
what it means to be like Christ	57%
reading the Bible	56%

n=520 U.S. practicing Christian fathers of sons, May 2020. Practicing Christians have attended a worship service within the past month and strongly agree that faith is very important in their lives.

and God and to live out the plan he has for them, you'd see a lot of hands go up. In fact, if someone you met said they've been effectively discipled by someone, you'd probably be suspicious simply because it's so rare.

Do you remember Jesus's words in Luke 6:40? The student who is fully trained will be like the master. Being discipled is nothing more or less than being trained to become like Jesus.

In order to help Nate understand the importance of being a good disciple, I curated some questions for him that we worked through together. Here they are.

Who is God? What comes into our minds when we think about God is the most important thing about us. And you'd be amazed at how much moral therapeutic deism is floating around in the minds of young people who are aware of only half of the attributes of God. They have a distorted image of God and don't know who he is. Nate and I spent a lot of time going through books in small doses, always trying to get closer to an answer to the key question, Who is God?

What is the gospel? This is the second question we tackled. *Gospel*, as you may know, means "good news," and this phrase carries some assumptions. First, it's news, which means you have to find out about it—you don't just know it. Second, it's good. I've been grateful for the churches, camps, events, and mentors that have impacted Nate's life, but I wanted to look my son in the eye and share the good news of the gospel of Jesus Christ with him myself.

What is the biblical story? The Bible can be a big, confusing book, and there are so many aspects of it we can help walk our teenagers through to help them gain understanding: the creation, the fall, the rise of the patriarchs, the exodus, the establishment of the children of Israel, the prophets, the kings, the rebellion, all of the things leading up to Jesus's arrival, and the redemption and restoration of all things. I spent time helping Nate understand the biblical story. My overarching goal behind exploring this question was getting Nate to the place where he knew these things himself. Not because I told him. Not because he heard about them. But because he actually did his own reading, thought about these things, and came to his own conclusions.

How do I read the Bible? Nate and I went through the acronym TIME: truth, insights, mission, and encounter. This helped him to put the Bible in context, to see how to study different parts of the Bible, and to learn how to hear the voice of the Holy Spirit, how to resist temptation, and how to obey God. During this time, I also introduced him to the spiritual disciplines. I wanted him, on his own, to discover how to find God's will, how to make decisions, how to guide his life, and how to share his faith.

One of the highlights of this time was Nate's decision to get baptized.

"Do you want to be a follower of Jesus?" I asked Nate after we had gone through this material. "Do you understand the gospel?"

"Yes."

"Do you understand the biblical story? Are you committed to walking with God and practicing the ways of Jesus?"

"Yes, I am."

"Do you want to do God's will?"

"Yeah, Dad, I do."

"Then do you think it's time to respond in baptism?"

"Yes, Dad; I'm excited to do this."

Nate's baptism was a beautiful moment in our journey together. I led him through the baptism liturgy our church uses, and I've got to tell you, it was hard! I cried like a little baby. I still get choked up just thinking about it—hearing my son say he renounced Satan and all the evil forces of darkness that try to pull him away from the love of God. I've got a great photo of Nate coming up out of the water and being hugged and our congregation just cheering him on.

Please, don't outsource the discipleship of your kids to their youth group. I love student ministry, and they can be wonderful partners, but God has given you a sacred responsibility to disciple your kids, to help them walk that path, and to give them the tools they need.

Role #2: Lover

I consciously put this role right after being a disciple of Jesus, because I knew Nate was in the middle of puberty and was paying attention to girls more than he ever had before. I wanted him to feel confident in his understanding of women and what it looked like to honor and respect them. We talked about the beauty and wonder of what a woman is, the importance of treating women with dignity, and the idea of being colaborers in the kingdom. I didn't want him to take a cultural view of women but to understand the privilege and wonder of having a relationship with someone of the opposite sex. We talked about the purpose and joy of marriage and how to prepare himself to become a man of commitment and faithfulness.

After talking about the wonder of women, we did a whole section on the nature of his changing body. This wasn't the

Relating to Women

While sex and dating should certainly not be the only ways women and men relate to one another, they are a hugely important aspect of teen and adult mixed-gender relationships. Yet just half of U.S. dads (57% of practicing Christians) say they've talked with their sons ages thirteen and older about these topics. Just one-third have discussed sexual consent and sexism with their teen or young-adult son.

U.S. FATHERS OF SONS 13 AND OLDER

sex	54%
dating	52%
consent	40%
sexism	36%

n=437 U.S. fathers of sons ages 13 and older, May 2020.

sex talk but more an acknowledgment that his body was morphing from a boy into a man. I wanted him to be aware of his physical desires and drives, and how they would manifest themselves in his day-to-day life. We talked about dating and the temptations that come with it. We talked about sex and the cultural distortions of sexuality and love, and we watched a few movies that gave us positive and negative representations of love. We talked about masturbation, porn, and rape culture. We talked about objectification and violence against women, and how these are inappropriate ways of interacting with women, especially as a Christ follower.

We talked about biblical accountability and the importance of bringing our sin to confession rather than hiding it in shame. We discussed the effects of porn and why it is the new drug. In light of this, I had Nate listen to a couple of podcasts and interviews with former porn addicts and the effects it had on their biology, their neurology, and their relationships. My goal here was to help him understand that porn is an objectifying illusion, it's not real, and it leads to only harmful outcomes.

We also got into some very practical topics, like how to know if a girl likes you, how to approach a girl you like, and how to ask her out on a date. We talked about planning out a date and how to show a girl a respectful good time, and also how to approach a girl's mother, father, aunt, or uncle with respect and confidence.

At the end of our conversations, Nate felt very confident and no longer like he was going into his adolescence completely blind when it came to women—how to treat them, how to view them, and how to interact with them.

Role #3: Leader

I wanted to help my son understand what godly leadership looks like, and one of the books I used to walk him through this was *Raising a Modern-Day Knight* by Robert Lewis. One of the definitions from this book that I love has to do with being a man: "A man accepts responsibility, rejects passivity, leads courageously, and lives for the greater reward."[1]

Nate and I spent time talking about the importance of accepting responsibility for our lives and choices and not passively blaming our circumstances. How many times do you see men trying to shrug off the consequences of their actions? And how refreshing is it when something goes wrong and you see the person involved own up to their role in that? Accepting responsibility is so important in growing up.

How many men do you know who are passive, who let others go first, who hang back and wait to see what's going to happen? We talked about the importance of rejecting passivity and taking the lead. The key insight to impart here is that passivity leads to pain. Life will keep moving forward, and choosing to do nothing is as large a decision with real-world consequences as choosing to take action. Fear-based passivity must be acknowledged, confronted, and pushed out of a young man's life.

Speaking of leadership, Nate and I also went through John Maxwell's *Leadership Bible* and *The 20 Most Important Minutes in a Leader's Day*. I recommend always keeping a lookout for particular authors or themes that resonate with your son. We ended up making our way through many of John Maxwell's books because they resonated with Nate a lot. He and I also dove into James Kouzes and Barry Posner's book *The Challenge of Leadership* and their five exemplary behaviors of leadership. This whole leadership section was so rewarding.

Whenever we finished a book, I took Nate out for dinner to celebrate his progress, and I gave him experiments where he could demonstrate his newfound leadership skills.

Role #4: Warrior

Men need a cause. A cause is bigger than a vision, more expansive than a strategy, and more long-lasting than a season. It's larger than a fight.

Sadly, most men don't have a cause. But they still have instincts and desires to give themselves to something that matters. Sadly, most of this energy and possibility is channeled into video games these days. Instead of figuring out how to make a difference in their actual lives, men resort to on-screen substitutes that give them the same adrenaline rush, sense of accomplishment, and mission to have these needs met. This is one reason I think you have to be careful about how much your son plays video games—they are very good at providing a false sense of accomplishment.

Men ache to master something, to be seen as strong and to receive honor and respect, and because it is so hard to attain this in real life, many of us default to chasing these things in the digital realm, because the wonderful myth of video games is that you can conquer the world.

But they're pretend worlds.

I wanted Nate to have a cause in real life. I wanted him to be a warrior.

We began by talking about fighting for the truth—also called *apologetics*. I tried to help Nate understand what it looks like to fight in forms outside of raw strength—what about fighting through legal capital, or authority, or privilege, or community action? These are all weapons that can be used in a battle, so how can we bring them to bear in a cause to advance truth and justice in the world?

We talked about mental toughness, about strengthening the mind through discipline and resolve and determination.

We talked about physical toughness, something most men are obsessed with. Think about how many times a man looks at himself in the mirror—after he wakes up, before he gets in the shower, when he gets out of the shower. There's something about being physically fit that appeals to us, so I tried to teach Nate about the gift of that—learning to fight through pain, being mentally tough, and acquiring physical skills over time.

The primary way we developed this was by enrolling him in Tae Kwon Do, a discipline he trained in for years and in which he eventually earned his black belt. It was an incredible process of learning how to leverage his physical strength and discipline his body—and learning the role of discipline in becoming good at something. Nate and I also lifted weights together, and I practiced with him when he was on sports teams.

I wanted him to be physically strong and to learn about his role as a warrior.

Role #5: Brother

At the heart of the role of being a brother is the knowledge of how to be in community. Can you identify true and false friends? Can you learn how to forgive? How do you confront someone without being judgmental?

I tried to give Nate a framework for confronting his friends well, building a brotherhood, and having a godly good time. We dove into the difference between a circle of concern and a circle of influence—who do you care about versus who is shaping you?

If we look around, I think it's clear that most men fail when it comes to creating a community of brotherhood. We hide, withdraw, or use power to control those around us. I wanted to impart to Nate an understanding of brotherhood and friendship by exploring the concepts of forgiveness, confrontation, encouragement, and building a sense of togetherness.

Much of our exploration of this role ended up as a kind of ongoing question-and-answer session where I asked him things like:

Where are you stuck at school?
Where are you having a tough time?
Are there bullies around?
What are you responding to?
What are you learning from your friends?
Where do you see your friends heading?

Loneliness among men is almost at epidemic proportions. Men no longer seem to have spaces where they can open their hearts without judgment, know how to be vulnerable with their pain, and stand beside each other in real support. Learning to develop male friendships during adolescence and carry those relational skills forward will lay a deep foundation of brotherhood for the years to come.

Role #6: Wise Man

We live in a culture of fools. Men need to learn to become wise.

Nate and I used the book of Proverbs as our foundation for talking about living out the role of a wise man, discussing the traits of the foolish and the wise and identifying both in our culture. We dug into the practice of stewarding our time—wasting it, investing it, using it, spending it, and redeeming it. We did the same with money.

For example, I walked Nate through the idea of paying $5 for a latte, and how much that $5 could become through the years with compound interest. What if we drank black coffee instead or made the latte ourselves? How would that impact us in the long term? We talked about many little things like this that I think very few people think through. I know I didn't, when I was younger. I dropped out of high school at age sixteen and made good money as a young man, yet no one ever sat down with me and talked about how to have a budget or how to save. I bought a house, but only because my boss said to me, "Tyson, you're wasting too much money. Buy a house. Develop an asset." It sounded like a great idea to me, so I did it.

I didn't want my son to have the same lack of understanding. Nate and I read a series of books together about money and tried to better understand its traps and its possibilities.

EXPLORING THESE ROLES together can be an incredibly rich time. Seeing your son grow physically, spiritually, mentally, and emotionally as a skillful young man mastering the roles of life well is one of the greatest joys a father can have. It can also be challenging because this kind of development takes time. It can feel overwhelming to work through all of this on your own as a dad, so utilize your tribe. Bring in the people around you to sit down with your son as mentors.

Think about those in your life who, from your perspective, embody these roles and are capable of providing input into them. Who do you think could speak into identifying a fool versus a wise person? Who has accumulated money with integrity? Who fights for a cause, living their life in a way that matters? Who do you see as someone who has a healthy relationship with women, loving their wife well and respecting the other women they interact with?

Use your community. Use the media at your disposal. Read biographies. Dig into Scripture.

You have more tools than you think. And as you work through this with your son, you'll realize that you are making progress too.

QUESTIONS *to* Think About

☞ What are some things you do yourself, instead of involving your kids, because you know you can do it faster? Could there be opportunities in these spaces for them to learn valuable things?

☞ Do you think the six roles I listed are comprehensive, or are there other archetypal roles that come to mind?

☞ Which roles do you think you are strong at, and which are more challenging for you?

INTENTIONAL STEPS

Write down each of the six roles and then list out various ways you can introduce them to your son. What activities would you like to do? What books would be good to read? What concepts do you want to dig into?

Use the following to design a process to help your son master the roles of manhood. What do you want him to know, be, and do as a leader of others?

Scriptures to study:

Biographies to read:

Movies to watch:

Trips to take:

Places to visit:

People to talk to:

Cohort/solo events to attend:

Marking the moment and celebrating growth:

CHAPTER TWELVE

Self-Discovery

Listen to your life. See it for the fathomless mystery it is. In the boredom and pain of it, no less than in the excitement and gladness: touch, taste, smell your way to the holy and hidden heart of it, because in the last analysis all moments are key moments, and life itself is grace.

FREDERICK BUECHNER

THE PRINCIPLE

Our goal as fathers is to help our sons discover who God has made and called them to be. We are not to make them in our own image but to help them along the path of grace so that they are renewed in the image of their Creator. This will bring them confidence and vision to move forward.

ONE OF THE GREATEST CHALLENGES young people face is figuring out who they are. The uncertainty and pain of this is particularly acute during adolescence. Yet conversations around identity rarely get the same traction with men as they do with women. Whenever I'm around women's ministries, they seem to be digging into this idea of identity, and they are good at discovering who they are.

On the other hand, most men don't have a clue who they are or who they're supposed to be. Which means our sons don't know how to become who they're supposed to be, and that leads to a huge area of confusion.

You can help eliminate this confusion for your son by walking through this chapter of self-discovery with him.

Nate and I began this part of the journey later in his high school years, and I recommend you don't do it much earlier than eleventh grade. Our approach was simple, and it boiled down to this: Nate took any and every personality and skills test I could get my hands on.

That's it.

I wanted him to have world-class insight into who he was, what his strengths were, what his spiritual gifts were, and what his weaknesses were—a cornucopia of self-discovery. At the end of it he had the language to talk about his personality—the paradigms, the pictures, the charts, and the reports on what made him who he was.

Here are the various tests and evaluations I walked him through.

The Enneagram

One of the simplest and most insightful personality tests you can take is the Enneagram. It can give you insight into your motivations, your fears, and the things that drive you. And it can be a strong framework through which you can view and understand not only yourself but those around you. It has brought nuance and depth to our understanding of each other as father and son.

What I like most about this one is that it shows you what you're like when you're healthy and integrated and what you're like when you're struggling and falling apart under stress. You get a good picture of the best and worst of yourself.

On the Enneagram, I'm a four with a three wing, which basically means I'm either really driven to be special or I'm special because I'm really driven. I still haven't quite nailed that one down. Your number will give you insight into how you parent, how you live your life, and how you interact with others, which is why I wanted Nate to take the test, find out his number, and begin exploring what the Enneagram had to teach him about himself.

Everyone in our family took the test, which was great, but Nate and I dug into it even deeper together. We had a ton of conversations about our numbers, and once we discovered Nate's number, it gave us a lot of insight into our relationship and our shared interests, and it helped us to bond around aesthetics, emotions, heart, and our passions.

As we spoke more about what his number meant, it was so funny because he would burst out laughing. "This just makes so much sense," he'd say. The Enneagram has a particular ability to make you feel like someone has been following you around, recording your behavior, and is now reporting on what they've been watching. It's just so spot-on.

StrengthsFinder

I'm a huge believer in StrengthsFinder. We live in a culture that's obsessed with talking about weaknesses, diagnosing illnesses, and identifying problems, but there seems to be very limited language for talking about our strengths.

Enter the StrengthsFinder test.

One of the things I love about this program is that it has a specific version for young people, in which they modify the language and provide different insights, which was so encouraging because at the end of it, Nate was able to say, "Here are five things I'm really good at." And it gave him some areas of confidence and places for him to focus on forming competence. It also showed him that God had sovereignly deposited areas of strength in him, literally created him to do specific things, and seeing this gave Nate the courage to step up and say, "Let me have a go at that," or, "I'm wired for that and I want to give it a try."

Finding your strengths can be a big step in the direction of knowing yourself.

Spiritual Gifts

Spiritual gifts assessments seem to mostly be reserved for adults; I personally know very few parents who have taken their kids through any kind of formal spiritual gifts assessment. But if we want our children to own their experience in the church, as opposed to simply being consumers who attend based on preference, this is so important.

I've heard a fair number of Christians look down on this idea of exploring our spiritual gifts, saying that the assessments aren't helpful or that it's a pointless exercise. But I say the tests currently available are better than nothing, and even if they don't lead to conclusive findings, they create a helpful starting point for good conversations about how we as Christians will engage with the church.

Nate enjoyed finding out what his spiritual gifts are, what they reveal about him, and where he might find the most joy in service to the church. He liked discovering a few different areas in which he might be naturally gifted and could contribute to the larger ministry of the church. We do our kids a disservice when we fail to help them know how God has made them to serve and thrive in the church.

APEST Test

Also in the realm of discovering spiritual gifts, the APEST Test is an Ephesians 4 test you can take online for $10, and it puts you into one of five categories: apostolic, prophetic, evangelistic, shepherding, or teaching. It helps you answer the questions, What sort of role might I play within the church? What section in the body of Christ am I going to be most helpful in? Pioneering? Hearing from God? Spending time with the lost? Caring for people? Teaching?

Knowing this has helped Nate think a little more about how he can effectively plug into the mission of his local church.

Myers-Briggs

Most people have heard about the Myers-Briggs personality profile test, but relatively few seem to have taken it. It can be helpful in bringing you to a more objective understanding of whether you are an introvert or an extrovert. Are you a thinker or do you act intuitively?

This test was especially helpful for Nate, and I feel like having him take the test gave him a tremendous head start in terms of vocational discernment as well as a valuable self-awareness that will help him relate better with those who manage him and enable him to work better under someone else's authority. Nate now has the chance to tell a future supervisor, "Hey, just so you know, this is my personality, this is how I work best, and this is how I respond to certain situations." It's so proactive.

Birkman Test

We loved all of these various tests and exercises, and each one helped us learn so much about Nate and, more importantly, gave him insight into his own identity. But what felt like the crown jewel of all the tests was the Birkman Test, which has to be administered by a trained Birkman professional in order to get the right yield from it. It's very comprehensive, with the goal of providing genuine vocational discernment from a Christian perspective.

It helps answer questions such as, What part of our culture should you consider serving in? How do you find your place in the larger kingdom of God? What is your mission in the world? This was amazing because it gave Nate some good parameters to move forward with.

One of the lies we tell our young people is that they can be whatever they want to be, but in reality we are limited by our talents, our temperaments, our personalities, and even our physical makeup. If you are four-foot-eleven, you're going to struggle to make it to the NBA. That's just a fact. So, how can we help our young people embrace the natural limits they've been handed and walk in the direction of their strengths? How can we help them see God's fingerprints and God's design and then move forward with those in mind?

The Birkman Test is very, very helpful for this.

A person in our community who is a trained Birkman assessment advisor took Nate through the test and then met

Vocational Discipleship

In Barna president David Kinnaman's 2019 book *Faith for Exiles*, he explores five practices that help young people develop resilient, lasting faith into adulthood. One of these is vocational discipleship, in which parents and churches are intentional about helping teens and young adults connect their career aspirations to their Christian faith. Looking at a group called "resilient disciples"—who are defined by their commitment to Jesus, involvement in a faith community, reliance on the Scriptures, and passion to connect the gospel with their lives—Barna found they are much more likely than other young adults with a Christian background to strongly agree with these calling- and vocation-related statements.

CONNECTING FAITH AND VOCATION:
A HALLMARK OF RESILIENT DISCIPLESHIP

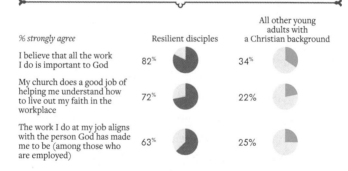

% strongly agree	Resilient disciples		All other young adults with a Christian background	
I believe that all the work I do is important to God	82%		34%	
My church does a good job of helping me understand how to live out my faith in the workplace	72%		22%	
The work I do at my job aligns with the person God has made me to be (among those who are employed)	63%		25%	

n=1,514 U.S. 18- to 29-year-olds who grew up as Christians, February 2018. David Kinnaman and Mark Matlock, *Faith for Exiles: 5 Ways for a New Generation to Follow Jesus in Digital Babylon* (Grand Rapids: Baker Books, 2019).

with him one-on-one. They worked through his results to-gether, and then my wife and I were given the results so that we could continue the conversation with Nate. It provided such good material to work through.

I began having informed conversations with Nate that weren't just based on opinions. I could ask him questions like, "Nate, based on what you've learned about yourself, what do you think God may be calling you to do with your life? What sort of vocation do you think you should take? What college might be the right one to help you move toward this vocation?"

I wasn't saying, "Well, Nate, as I see it, you should do this or that." We all had the same facts and the same informa-tion, and we could plan with intentionality and knowledge. This became more and more valuable as we approached the time when Nate would be leaving the house and starting life on his own.

One thing I need to note as you begin this process of discern-ment and help your teenager move into a time of self-discovery: it's important to honor the preferences and conclusions they have and arrive at. Often as parents we think we always know best, so we try to steer our kids in a particular direction. It's so easy to dismiss their tastes, preferences, and affinities.

Maybe they come home one day and say, "I like this par-ticular band," and you respond by saying, "Oh, that music is rubbish. Why do you like that?" No, when they're learning what they like, honor that, and then incorporate the things they like into the gifts you give them, the things you affirm for them, and the experiences you create for them. Recognizing that your kids have valid preferences is crucial during this time period.

What do they like to read, watch, and listen to? Cheer them on! Encourage them to continue developing their own interests, and you'll see their personalities evolve in wonderful, healthy, and exciting ways.

Think about these tests and personality profiles. Think about how frequently you'd like to do them and on what kind of time frame, and how you'll celebrate and dig deeper as the results come in.

Helping Nate come to a better understanding of who he was became one of the most wonderful parts of this whole experience, and watching him grow into that has been one of the great joys of my life.

QUESTIONS *to* Think About

☞ How well do you know yourself? How has this self-awareness helped you make important decisions in life?

☞ What are some of the big decisions you see your teenager needing to make in the coming years, and how do you hope that better self-awareness will help him make better decisions?

INTENTIONALSTEPS

When will you begin this process of testing and self-evaluations?

What are the specific tests you plan on having your child take?

Who will help you walk through these various tests?

What is your plan for exploring the results of these tests?

Use the following questions to help process each of these tests with your son.

Results:

What does this mean?

What does it explain?

What does it have implications for?

What does it help others know?

CHAPTER THIRTEEN

The Arc of Life

There is a time in the life of every boy when he for the first time takes the backward view of life. Perhaps that is the moment when he crosses the line into manhood.

SHERWOOD ANDERSON

THE PRINCIPLE

Young men rarely think long and hard about the decisions and directions they want their lives to take. The horizon of their thinking often extends to the end of their current season and the start of the next. But wise men understand the arc and seasons of a life and seek to live well in each season to minimize regret and maximize joy.

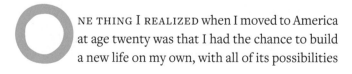

ONE THING I REALIZED when I moved to America at age twenty was that I had the chance to build a new life on my own, with all of its possibilities and perils. But what I didn't know was how to live that life well over the course of time. What's the big-picture perspective of what a life is supposed to look like? How do we navigate the complexities of each season of life, overcome its challenges, and savor its rewards? We live in a culture where everything has to be immediate; it's a culture of the *now*, where few people want to make decisions and investments that will take years to pay off. This means that many of us find ourselves moving through life without any idea of where we should be or what we should be doing at that particular point in life. We end up in disordered chronologies, going from one decade to the next without any sense of meaning.

I'm not trying to impose some sort of hard line over life, but we are called to live intentionally, and if we don't consciously choose our lives and the seasons we are in, the culture will do whatever it wants with us. We'll easily drift from season to season. This chronological confusion can lead to deep regret and aimlessness.

That's a recipe for getting lost.

This is why I decided that one thing I definitely wanted to give Nate during his adolescence was exposure to all of the seasons and stages of life. We have a responsibility to help our children understand the arc of life, along with their corresponding temptations and joys. This way, they're not blindsided by whatever their next new stage of life has to offer.

We need to explain the temptations and joys of high school, a time that is primarily about *exposing* us to life. This is where so many of our firsts happen; it's a season of exploration, of being exposed to beauty and wonder and heartache and pain. High school is about experiencing the euphoria of teenage life—don't close off your options, don't say no, don't say you don't like something. Experience what's out there.

After that comes college, and we need to explain the temptations and joys of that time of life too. College is primarily about *learning*—you have a bit of clarity about what direction you'd like to go, but you're learning more about it, learning more about God, learning more about yourself.

And then your twenties come. What a season! They're all about *growing*, figuring out who you are as a person and getting better at that. It's a decade of intense growth. Your thirties are about *editing*, because you're finally getting a sense of what your cause is. You begin shutting off certain life options because you want to focus, and you prune out the things in your life that you realize don't matter anymore.

Your forties are about *mastering*. You still have energy, and it combines with a bit of idealism about how your life and the world should be. You have a cause, and you're getting better at it, and you're going for it. In your forties, you emerge as a master in your craft.

The temptations and the joys of your fifties revolve around *harvesting*, a decade when you can hopefully begin bringing in the results of decades of previous life's work. Your sixties are all about *guiding*. You're beginning to turn your attention away from yourself and taking notice of the generations coming after you. Some in their sixties may find a new desire to help guide younger folks through these life stages.

Your seventies are about *imparting*, or consciously taking everything that has been deposited in your life and pouring it out for others, preparing to leave your legacy and history behind for others. Your eighties are about *savoring*. Your nineties are about *preparing* to reach the finish line, closing up loose ends, and making sure you are ready to meet your Maker.

I know these are very general guidelines, but I think that a life following this arc would be a good life, a meaningful life. And I think there's huge value in helping the young people around us realize that life, for most of us, will be long, and we need to think about how we're going to navigate these years, these stages.

And so, I introduced Nate to arc-of-life interviews.

Who do you know who you believe has an incredible amount of wisdom, someone who could talk through the key temptations, lessons, and joys of each stage of life? Who do you know who got college right, or who, as they reflect on their twenties, can say their twenties were a rich time of life? Who got their thirties right? Their forties? Their fifties? Who is in their sixties and is really investing in younger people? Whom do you know in their seventies who is pouring themselves out? Who in their eighties is savoring life? Who in their nineties is preparing well to meet their Maker?

Meaningful Intergenerational Relationships

A practice of resilient discipleship explored in Kinnaman's book *Faith for Exiles* is forming life-giving, generative friendships with older and younger Christians.

FORGING INTERGENERATIONAL FRIENDSHIPS: A HALLMARK OF RESILIENT DISCIPLESHIP

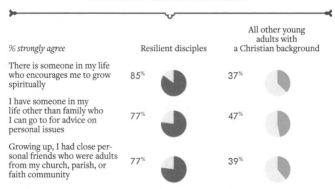

	Resilient disciples	All other young adults with a Christian background
% strongly agree		
There is someone in my life who encourages me to grow spiritually	85%	37%
I have someone in my life other than family who I can go to for advice on personal issues	77%	47%
Growing up, I had close personal friends who were adults from my church, parish, or faith community	77%	39%

n=1,514 U.S. 18- to 29-year-olds who grew up as Christians, February 2018. David Kinnaman and Mark Matlock, *Faith for Exiles: 5 Ways for a New Generation to Follow Jesus in Digital Babylon* (Grand Rapids: Baker Books, 2019).

THE CONNECTION BETWEEN INTERGENERATIONAL FRIENDSHIPS AND MEN'S WELL-BEING

% very satisfied among practicing Christian men

● friends of a different age group ○ no intergenerational relationships

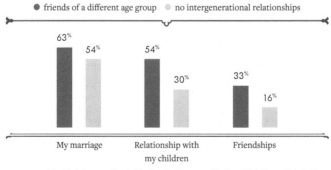

	My marriage	Relationship with my children	Friendships
friends of a different age group	63%	54%	33%
no intergenerational relationships	54%	30%	16%

n=1,000 practicing Christian men 18 and older, October 8–21, 2019. *Five Essentials to Engage Today's Men: Conversations Every Church Should Have about How Men Connect with Their Purpose, with Others & with Their Faith* (Ventura, CA: Barna Group, 2020).

Prepare your son to meet one-on-one with these individuals, maybe over coffee or a meal. Help him come up with questions to ask, things that will help him learn from these people about what makes each particular stage of life rich and rewarding. What warnings can they pass on? What themes have they seen throughout life?

I remember one specific meeting Nate had with a close family friend. This man's words will hopefully resonate with Nate for the rest of his life.

"Nate," he said, "you have this huge safety net under your life. You've got to be willing to risk everything, because you can."

This friend is in his forties, one of the most successful people I've ever met, and his words had a huge impact on Nate.

These meetings will be a real gift. These people will give your son real perspective on life, and the conversations they have with him will give you more things to discuss as you continue along this path.

But don't expect every meeting to go smoothly or to provide immediate results. A few of the meetings were a little awkward for Nate, and much of the wisdom he received from these meetings has yet to bear fruit. The real value is in the seeds that have been sown, seeds that will hopefully come back to Nate in the years to come.

Hebrews 13:7 comes to mind: "Remember your leaders, who spoke the word of God to you. Consider the outcome of their way of life and imitate their faith."

That's really what we're trying to do here: introduce our sons to people of consequence who will give them a model for what that stage of their lives might look like.

QUESTIONS *to* Think About

☞ What stage of life are you currently in?

☞ How have people in other stages of life spoken into your existence and helped you navigate or prepare for an upcoming stage?

INTENTIONAL STEPS

Make a list that includes at least one person from each of these stages in life for your son to meet with.

Help your son come up with a list of questions that will generate the kind of discussion you're looking for—namely, dialogue that explores the joys and temptations of each stage of life.

Sixties: Imparting to the Next Generation

Possible people to interview:

What did you most enjoy about your sixties? Why?

What are three of your favorite memories from your sixties?

What are your biggest regrets of your sixties?

If you had your sixties to do again, what would you do differently?

What things must I absolutely get right in my sixties?

What things must I absolutely avoid in my sixties?

If you could speak into my life, knowing what you know about me, what would you say?

CHAPTER FOURTEEN

The Gap Year

The real risk is not changing. I have to feel that I'm after
something. It's the striving, man, it's that I want.

JOHN COLTRANE

THE PRINCIPLE

*Young men need a liminal space where they are removed from the
normal rhythm and routine of life and given time and opportunity
to see what is inside them. They need space to encounter those
who have grown up in completely different cultural contexts and
bond with other men. In modern life, nothing does this quite as
well as a gap year.*

T HE PLANS WE'RE GOING TO TALK ABOUT in this
chapter assume a few things: one, your teenager has
graduated or is about to graduate from high school;

two, you've marked that moment properly or are planning to do so; and three, you're in the final stages of this journey you've been taking together.

This time period is crucial. You've made it this far. Commit to yourself that you're going to end really, really well.

As Nate entered his senior year, I went to him with a request: "Would you consider taking a gap year between high school and college?"

I felt like a gap year could play an important part in his preparation to enter the next stage of his life. I became interested in the concept of a gap year partially because I grew up in Australia; it's more common there for teens to take a year off after high school prior to starting college. Also, as someone who has served in youth ministry and discipled a lot of teens in the United States, I had seen what happened when they headed straight from high school to college. I felt like so many of them would have benefited from a larger liminal space, a transitional event or process that would give them more time to get ready for college, not necessarily academically but emotionally. They needed time to mature.

I thought of a specific handful of guys whom I had mentored through high school. I was their youth pastor and had been diligent and intense in training them during their senior year. We studied Grudem's *Systematic Theology*, going through the entire book. We regularly woke up at 4:00 a.m. to pray over their school. I'd poured into them, invested relationally into their lives, and had high hopes for them.

But during their first week of college, I received frantic calls from two of them. One had lost his virginity at a party, and the other had gotten radically drunk for the first time. They just weren't equipped; they were not prepared for what college was going to throw at them. They definitely could have used a bit of time between high school and college, but, like so many other kids at that age, they were itching to throw off the yoke of their parents and party. (Fortunately, both realized the intensity of temptation and turned to God, and now walk with him.)

And so, I felt a need to give my son a larger vision of the world before he entered college. I hoped it would provide Nate with greater insight into God's heart for him and others. I had two concrete goals for this gap year—first, that he would encounter the poor and realize in a visceral way that his life wasn't just about himself. Second, that he wouldn't jump on the career and success conveyor belt, the winner script, prey to an overwhelming feeling that he had to get ahead and he had to do it *now*. A lot of people carry an incredible amount of pressure into their college experience, simply because they don't have a bigger perspective, a more comprehensive understanding of the world and of themselves.

As we've already talked about, almost all formation pathways in other cultures involve some sort of quest or journey, such as the Mormons' mission trip and the Native American vision quest. There's something powerful about leaving home and seeing the world, then returning again in a different way. I wanted Nate to have that kind of a liminal year.

You're probably thinking, *You keep using that word* liminal. *What's that all about?*

According to Wikipedia, *liminality* is "the quality of ambiguity or disorientation that occurs in the middle stages of a rite of passage, when participants no longer hold their pre-ritual status but have not yet begun the transition to the status they will hold when the rite is complete."[1] They're in between. They're neither here nor there.

That's what liminal space is. It's when your son is no longer a high school student but also is not yet a college student, or a tradesperson, or a full-time employee. It's in this space that he has time to bring together all the things he's learned, get to know himself even better, and then take deliberate steps forward instead of simply charging ahead without thinking.

My wife and I spent time walking through this decision with our son. Why did we think it was important that he go on a pilgrimage? Why did we think it was important that he see the world? Why did we think it was important that his heart be irreparably broken for the global poor? Why did we think it was important that he see that the world is not just the America he grew up in? Getting to the heart of these "why" questions helped him to understand the importance of taking a gap year, and it also helped us with the next step, which was deciding what he should do during that year.

That was the next challenge: Where should he do this?

Now, the path we took might not be the right path for you and your son. I totally get that. You don't have to spend the kind of money we spent (more on that later), but I do believe that encouraging your child to take one year off between high school and college is a gift you can give them. It's an opportunity for them to step off the treadmill and make sure their foundation is firm.

I got on my creative, entrepreneurial hat and remembered I had a very close friend named Dave Blanchard who runs an organization called Praxis Labs. They have mentored dozens and dozens of nonprofit leaders from around the world, and I thought I could contact ten or eleven of these leaders and send Nate to a different country every month, interning at these various places. That way he could see the world.

I shared this idea with a friend of mine, and he said, "That problem has already been solved, Jon. Have you ever heard of the World Race or Adventures in Missions?"

"No."

"Google them," he said. "Just check them out."

I did, and I couldn't believe it. Adventures in Missions was an organization that, for over two decades, has been sending young adults around the world to do the exact program I was trying to create for Nate myself. They expose young people's hearts to the poor, give them a vision for the kingdom of God, break off the spirit of entitlement and selfishness that often exists at that age, and just get them ready to move into adulthood.

Nate made the final decision that joining this program was what he wanted to do, and he was going to travel and work through India, Nepal, Swaziland, and Guatemala for nine months during his gap year. The cost would be around $16,000 for the whole program: travel, insurance, food, everything.

Once he'd made this decision, it was time to enter the process of fundraising. This became a beautiful moment in and of itself. "Nate," I said, "you're going to see the body of Christ rally around you. You're going to find out personally about the generosity of the people of God." And that's exactly what happened. He was blown away by how much people believed in him, even people who had never met him but were touched by our ministry and wanted to support him. He went through a process of formation, prayer, gratitude, and seeing firsthand what God can do. That alone made taking a gap year worth it.

We're going to talk about money here for a moment, because I know some of you will initially feel discouraged about undertaking a gap year due to the cost of some of these programs. Think of it this way—you are, hopefully, starting this process with your son when he is twelve or thirteen years old. If you can put $100 back every month, over the course of five years that's $6,000. Combine that with money he can save himself and money you can raise from friends and family, and you will be surprised at the kind of gap year experience you can provide for your child.

Whatever you do, don't let the price of it overwhelm you. Prepare your heart now and prepare your wallet now. Most organizations have great tools to help you fundraise, and maybe you even have relationships with people around the world who can help lower the cost by providing your son with a place to stay or a base to work from. Customize it however you want, but know there is tremendous benefit in a gap year.

THE MORNING NATE LEFT was hard. The money had been raised, high school graduation had occurred, and his time had come. He was leaving our home. It was painful for my wife, and I definitely felt a mixed bag of emotions: pride, sadness, joy, heartache, and excitement. We set our alarms, Nate woke up and got ready, and he moved to the door with all of his possessions packed into two bags, leaving his home the same way I had left mine all those years before.

We got him an Uber, he climbed in, and off he went into the world to see its beauty and its terror.

Begin sowing this idea of doing a gap year into the mind of your teenager. Let him know early, "This is part of the path. This gap year will benefit you in ways you can't even imagine right now. You can choose where you go, and here are some things we want this time to accomplish for you."

THE SECOND PART of this liminal year is a father-son pilgrimage.

For our pilgrimage, Nate and I decided to hike the Camino de Santiago when he had returned from his travels. The Camino, also known in English as the Way of St. James, is a pilgrimage ending in the northwestern Spanish city of Santiago de Compostela that people have been taking for hundreds of years, and it is done not just for religious reasons but also often for personal clarity. Some people who hike the Camino are carrying the ashes of a loved one or are trying to work their way emotionally through some kind of difficulty. I've had several friends who hiked the trail and can barely share their experiences without fighting back tears.

It's a five-hundred-mile hike.

Our plan was to spend a month completing the Camino, and during that month we would recap everything he had learned on this path into manhood as well as what he'd learned on his gap year travels. It would be him and me on a pilgrimage, a physical representation of the journey he had been on. During this trip we had a daily discussion about the principles he had learned, the things he needed to process, and the path ahead. The trip ended up facilitating some of the greatest moments of my life, and we bonded at the primal level.

That summer Spain encountered a historic heat wave. Neither of us will forget walking twenty miles through the mountains in 105-degree heat or the blisters that became holes in my heels. This trip was the culmination of six years of time together, and it's something both of us will carry in our hearts.

Think through what this might look like for you and your son. Some people plan a weekend trip to see a sports game. Some go on extended wilderness treks. Whatever you do, beware the soul-sucking voice of reason. Make this trip unreasonable. People should be asking, *Who does that? Who takes a month and hikes across a country?*

It will be worth it. Every time you make an excuse, you conspire with mediocrity. The window of willingness may close in this season. Seize it while it's open.

I know that many of you are wondering, "How will I ever afford this?"

I am a pastor, and not at a church that teaches the prosperity gospel. Our vocation isn't known for the size of the salary. But with discipline and planning, this trip came together. And looking back, I have zero regrets at the sacrifices to make it happen.

Plan now, save now. Automate this trip into a special account so you don't even have to think about it.

A second question people often ask me is, "What if my son doesn't want to do this gap year thing?"

That's a valid question, and you can't frame it as something he has to do. That's not the point. But if you tee it up properly, sowing seeds well in advance, it won't take any convincing—he'll ache to do it.

"What if my son goes off the rails sometimes during these years? What if he doesn't want to walk with God?" Listen, these things happen. There are other ways to do gap years that aren't religiously oriented. But you will be amazed at what God can do with a heart over the course of a year, especially during a year when everything changes and they can get away from familiar things and see the world in a new light.

Start the conversation. Talk with your family about the impact a gap year can have.

WHEN NATE AND I reached the end of our father-son pilgrimage on the Camino, we stayed in a house on the beach, and it felt like we were at the edge of the world. The setting was heaven on earth—blue skies and green trees and this beautiful stretch of beach that was sheltered in a cove. We walked down an ancient path lined with old stone walls, all the way to the rocky shore. There, I read letters to Nate written by men who had been part of this long journey, men who had words for him of celebration and blessing. I also went through a blessing ceremony I had designed for him.

He walked out onto the sand in his swimsuit. He glanced back at me once, saluted, then ran into the water.

When he came walking back out, I shouted out to him.

"A man emerges from the ocean! Who is this man?"

It was my son, who had walked the ancient path from adolescence into adulthood with his head held high and his heart full of life.

QUESTIONS *to* Think About

☞ What are your thoughts (and concerns) about a gap year?

☞ What was your transition like from high school into whatever you did afterward, whether it was college, trade school, or employment? How do you think you could have benefited from taking some time off?

☞ How would your child benefit from that kind of liminal space?

INTENTIONALSTEPS

What are some ideas you have for a gap year and a father-son pilgrimage? Dream big and think about some of the details. When? How long? Where? How?

CHAPTER FIFTEEN

Ceremony of Welcome and Blessing

It's a blessed thing to love and feel loved in return.

E. A. BUCCHIANERI

THE PRINCIPLE

If a son does not receive blessing from his father, he will spend the rest of his life trying to earn that blessing. Creating a blessing ceremony will help cement our sons' identity and heal wounds they have suffered along the way. It is something only we as fathers can give to our sons.

WHEN I TALK WITH DADS who have adult children, I am so often struck by the pain and grief of regret that many of them carry for the way they have raised their kids. Many have said with tears in their eyes, "I would give anything to get that time back and invest in those years again."

But this will not be your story! You're being proactive, passionate, and diligent, and at great cost of time, energy, and resource allocation.

I respect you for choosing to take this path. You won't regret it.

TO CLOSE OUT THIS JOURNEY, think about how to create a ceremony to end this unforgettable phase of your son's life. It's not how we start but how we finish that marks a successful transition into manhood.

I have a deep conviction that we are created with a need for blessing. Just look at Genesis 1:28:

> God blessed them and said to them, "Be fruitful and increase in number; fill the earth and subdue it. Rule over the fish in the sea and the birds in the sky and over every living creature that moves on the ground."

We are created for blessing, and we cannot function without it. In fact, we are desperate for it. Remember the story of Jacob, who yearned for a blessing from his father and was so determined to get it that he stole from his brother, deceived his father, and spent his entire life running from the consequences? Blessing and cursing is one of the central themes of our lives, as I wrote about in my book *The Burden Is Light*.

I want to close out this journey you've gone on with your son with a blessing. You began this whole thing with an initiation ceremony, and there needs to be a meaningful blessing to mark its end. He needs you to officially welcome him into the community of men. He needs to know and carry the weight of the fact that you are proud of him. He needs to feel a sense of accomplishment; this path he walked means something, and he can now head into his adult life with your blessing.

Just like Jacob chased his father's blessing, so will your son chase yours if you don't give it to him. He'll enter into a life of deception and striving, thinking that if he sleeps with enough women or makes enough money, he's going to be worthy. Maybe he'll try to prove himself by chasing public attention or dominating others physically. But the Bible shows us that when we receive a blessing, it changes the nature of our lives. Working *from* a place of blessing leads to a completely different life than working *for* a blessing.

Let's bless our sons well so that they don't spend the rest of their lives looking for this in other places.

THE ENDING OF MATTHEW'S GOSPEL used to be my favorite: "Therefore go and make disciples of all nations, baptizing them in the name of the Father and of the Son and of the Holy Spirit" (28:19). There's something wonderful about that missional sending, isn't there? There's something beautiful about the end of the story not necessarily being the end of the story.

But more recently, my favorite ending of any of the Gospels is Luke's.

> When he had led them out to the vicinity of Bethany, he lifted up his hands and blessed them. While he was blessing them, he left them and was taken up into heaven. Then they worshiped him and returned to Jerusalem with great joy. And they stayed continually at the temple, praising God. (24:50–53)

Is that not a powerful image? "While he was blessing them." I don't know exactly how that played out—was he beamed up into the sky? Did he slowly fade from sight, entering into another realm? Whatever the case, that mental image of their friend and savior blessing them is such a beautiful one.

And it's because of this moment that we see the disciples of Christ in Acts operating *from* Jesus's blessing and not *for* Jesus's blessing. They were distributing what they already had, not out there working to earn something new. The same could be said of Jesus's life—he knew he had his Father's blessing from the very beginning, which meant he was free from the tyranny of seeking applause.

Send your son out of your home with your blessing in a way that is unmistakable to him, so he will never wonder if he has it or not.

IMAGINE THIS MOMENT.

Your son has returned from his gap year. He's received your family values, made the five shifts, thought through the defining moments of his life, mastered six roles of being a man, discovered who he is, seen the world, been through all of these incredible experiences, and now he's returned home.

"Dad, what's next?"

"Whatever happens next," you reply, "you're going to get my blessing and operate out of that for the rest of your life."

What a powerful moment.

When Nate reached this moment, we wanted to celebrate this massive landmark appropriately, so we gathered on the rooftop of our building with about sixty of his friends and family members. We showed a video celebrating his entire life, and we had people speak words of affirmation over him. And because one of the primary ways Nate connects with God is through worship, we gathered around him and sang songs of hope and deliverance over him, embodying that beautiful passage about the Lord "[rejoicing] over you with singing" (Zeph. 3:17).

It was a living parable of our heavenly Father's love and a profound reminder that even as Nate was transitioning into adulthood, he would never leave his heavenly Father's care.

Here are a few questions to consider when you're planning this ceremony of blessing.

What men should be there to bless your son? One of the things we did for Nate that was so powerful was gathering together the key men who had influenced his life. Maybe some of the men you invite are the ones your son interviewed. Maybe some are other dads who have played a part in his journey. Words from men of consequence, spoken at the right moment, can mark a young man's heart and mind.

Which friends should be there? It's important that your son's friends see that he is a blessed man, that he's heading into this next stage of life with the blessing of his community of men. It can be a good time for them to speak words of affirmation over him and empower him for what's next too.

What will you share? Think carefully about the things you plan on saying and the ways your words will send him out.

What gifts will you give him that will mark him forever? Consider the things that mean a lot to you, and explore the idea of giving your son various tokens that will help him carry with him some of the things he has learned.

I told Nate I would give him two more things when he completed this journey from childhood to adulthood. The first is a medal I'd had for years, a gift from the Daily Stoic, one that I'd occasionally take out and show him. Second, I would give him a maxed-out Roth IRA that's worth around $6,000. I wanted to give him this account so that as he gets older—twenty, thirty, forty, fifty, sixty, seventy years old—he will realize the long-term effect of compound interest. Hopefully he will see the investment that has been made in his life, and it will bear fruit over the course of his lifetime.

These are all questions I considered when it came time for Nate's ceremony of blessing, and I've seen some beautiful examples of fathers doing this, getting it right, and creating a deep moment their son will never forget. Done right, this ceremony of blessing will lead sons in their twenties, thirties, and forties to remain walking in the knowledge that their father is proud of them and they have what it takes.

Dallas Willard says, "Blessing is the projection of good into the life of another."[1]

My prayer as you do this is that your skillful blessing provides your son with a picture of the blessing our heavenly Father offers us in Christ, and that this becomes a tangible moment marked in your son's life when he learns to live not for blessing but from blessing.

QUESTIONS *to* Think About

☞ How have you spent your life seeking blessing?

☞ What would you like your son to know about the blessing you are sending him out with?

INTENTIONALSTEPS

Make a list of the people you'd like to be present at this ceremony of blessing.

Where would you like to have it?

What affirmations should be spoken?

What gifts should you give your child?

How could you make this an extraordinary night where he delights in, and receives, your blessing?

CHAPTER SIXTEEN

The Intentional Father

You don't raise heroes, you raise sons. And if you treat them like sons, they'll turn out to be heroes, even if it's just in your own eyes.

WALTER M. SCHIRRA SR.

The nature of impending fatherhood is that you are doing something that you're unqualified to do, and then you become qualified while doing it.

JOHN GREEN

WELL, HERE WE ARE.

You did it.

You're well on your way to putting this plan in place, and you're way ahead of the game. Your son will be a completely different person because of this work that you're doing.

If you are literally at the end of this path, maybe sending your son out on his gap year or putting together the ceremony of blessing, again, well done. What a moment! What a journey! The things you have done will stretch out in the decades, and even the generations, ahead of you. This work has eternal consequence.

It is part of my life vision that this kind of intentional discipleship of young people becomes a normal thing in the Christian tradition. Fathers or father figures pick up young men, love them, walk with them, and help them navigate the challenges, perils, complexity, blessings, and opportunity that come as they move from adolescence into adulthood.

Engaging in this kind of intentional path will impact more people than you and the young person you're walking alongside—you are going to inspire people around you to pick up their game too. And the young people who see you going through this with your son will want something greater. They'll want to be part of something like this. Your involvement will lead to cohorts all over the nation, which in turn will lead to God doing something significant in this next generation of men.

I'M HONORED YOU would let me join you for this important time in your lives.

If you're still exploring this idea of intentional fatherhood or only just beginning this journey with your son, let me say this: I know you may feel frustrated, overwhelmed, or even despondent. There are probably points in this book where you wish I'd gone into deeper detail, and other points where you thought I may have gone into too much detail. What I've tried to do is distill the core principles I encountered after years of research, reading, and exploring this with Nate.

I want to encourage you to innovate, improve, and make this journey even better than it currently is! I haven't figured this all out—not at all. I've just given it my best shot in hopes of raising my son without regret. But I'm sure that as you learn from my experiences and see how others are doing it, you'll want to tweak your approach, maybe even take it to another level.

Go for it!

Ramp it up!

Stir it up!

I can't wait to see how people take my ideas as a baseline and improve on them, adjust them, and innovate.

HERE ARE MY ANSWERS to a few common questions.

What was your daily ritual like? Nate and I met every day before school from 5:45 a.m. until about 6:30, depending on what we were going through at the time. This gave us some solid boundaries from the beginning—there is no formation without repetition and consistency. This morning time was the meat and potatoes of the entire journey.

We went to the same spot in the house every morning, pulled out whatever book we were working through, grabbed our pens and journals, and dug in.

If you do nothing else, have a morning ritual with your son. This will change everything.

What kind of books did you purchase? One thing I always encourage people to do is to buy the hardcover versions of the books you go through, if possible. I prefer digital books myself, but I wanted to create a legacy of artifacts that Nate would have, so we went through all the books in hardcover. He marked them up, underlined in them, and then kept them in the footlocker I gifted him at the beginning. I wanted him to leave home with a rich box full of wonderful things, including the books we studied.

What tangible things did you do that you found to be helpful? For one, we had a sign I bought that said, "What good shall I do this day?" and at the end of every morning session, we would tap the sign and ask each other to answer the question.

We also had a list of values we recited every day. As Nate walked out of the house every morning, he would say, "Strength, courage, mastery, honor, vision, passion, discipline, and risk." He carried those values on his lips and in his heart.

What if I can't meet every morning? I get it. Everyone's schedule is different. Sometimes I had to travel, and we often did our morning time on Skype or FaceTime. The key to the whole thing is consistency, and I tried to help him see this. I would often tell him, "Nate, before you were born, I was getting up early to seek God, and when you leave my home, I will still use this time to seek God. I want you to know that I'm bringing you into this important time I spend with God, and I hope you establish this habit in your own life."

Maybe you can't do it five days a week. Do what you can. Do something. Be intentional. Make it consistent, and stick with it. Find a rhythm that works for you. I will say that once a month is not enough, and once a week is probably not enough either. We live in a world bombarding us with information every single moment of the day—I think it's going to take more than weekly meetings to make a difference.

Barna has research that shows the typical young person is exposed to three thousand hours of formative content a year, and only 150 hours of explicitly Christian content in that same time. Who do you think is winning that war? Who do you think is having the largest formative influence?

Whatever the frequency, there is a lot of power in morning meetings.

How do you make the weekly man nights great? Schedule these nights and protect them. If you have to miss one, try to make it up. I always included great food, and that added to our enjoyment of the evening, plus I always tried to give Nate some input into the content of the evenings and what we'd be digging into. My goal was not to create lectures for these evenings. I wanted to have insightful questions that turned into good conversations.

Here's one example of something we did: when we were talking about the beauty and strength of man, we'd watch one episode of *Band of Brothers* each week and then we'd eat at a different barbecue restaurant around New York City. *Band of Brothers* and barbecue.

Beware the soul-sucking voice of reason, but also don't feel pressure to make every single evening the biggest thing ever—that's a sure path to burnout. Just make it a good night.

How much of this process do you share on social media? This is such a relevant question, and something important for you to consider in this day and age, when everything is shared on Facebook, Twitter, or Instagram. Sometimes we can feel the impulse to share but we really shouldn't. Why? For one, the natural reaction of our society, when they see male formation, is to mock it. "Oh, looks like you're doing your man time or whatever." That kind of response can be really deflating, so Nate and I often tried to do our thing in secret.

I did share a lot, mostly because I wanted to encourage other men to up their game. I wanted to model that it's possible to invest more time and intentionality into the lives of our young people. But there's a ton I didn't share. I believe that male formation happens best when there's an element of secrecy around it. Even in our own home, there is a lot that my wife and daughter didn't know that we did.

How can I compile all that we're doing into one central place? One thing I want to encourage you to do is document the journey. Having the video footage of Nate's initiation when he was thirteen, wide-eyed and bushy-tailed, compared to the young man, taller than me, who came walking back up from the water after our trek on the Camino de Santiago—that's a wonderful thing. If you can gather some videos, photos, and documents created during your journey together, it can lend tremendous power to the whole thing, especially when you arrive at the end of it and prepare to send your son out into the world.

There are a few different ways you can do this. For me, I simply created a file on my computer and dumped it all in there. At the end of Nate's journey, I could pull some things from my files, curate them, and show him some beautiful moments from this amazing time we had together.

This seems like a lot of work. I'm not sure I can commit to all of this. Don't be overwhelmed. You can do this. Do what you can, not what you can't. Be consistent. Be purposeful. Your son's eighteenth birthday may seem like a long way off, but believe me, it will come in no time, and then your time with him in your own home will be over. Get a tribe of men around you for support, create a brotherhood, and utilize the resources in your community.

If you stumble, if you stop doing it for a time, shake it off and begin again. Maybe you get distracted and miss a month . . . who cares? Declare a reinitiation over dinner and jump back in. If you're driving on the highway and you get a flat tire, do you pull out a gun and shoot your remaining three good tires? No! You replace the flat and get back on the road.

Don't be discouraged by occasional lapses. This journey is going to matter. There will be very few things in your life that you're going to want to get right as much as raising your son.

LET'S NOT BE A GENERATION of fathers who push this crisis off to the next generation. Let's be fathers who release blessing and not brokenness, favor and not curses. Resolve in your spirit to do this with intensity and intentionality.

You can do this.

I want to close out this book by praying for you. Can I do that? I don't know where you are as you're reading this, but if possible, will you put your hands out and accept that what I pray will be deposited into your life? Whatever wisdom I have, receive it.

Let me pray for you.

Father, I come into your presence right now, into the throne room of God, and I want to bring my brothers who are reading this along with me. I thank you that we can call you our Father and that we can access your mercy, grace, and help in time of need.

Lord God, release the power of the Holy Spirit into the lives of the men reading. I want to pray that you will stir up their imagination, that you will fan into flame the gifts of

God within them, and that whatever they've been neglecting from their own story would be drawn back out and they would utilize it.

Whatever talents they have buried out of fear, I speak your Word that they would dig that back up and put it back into the market and get a return on the inheritance you've entrusted to them.

I pray that as they embark on this journey of intentional fatherhood, you would break off any generational drama that's seeking to flood into the lives of their sons. I pray that would be blocked and that, instead, blessing would flow.

Lord, I pray you would give us all the keys to our sons' hearts. Turn fathers' hearts back to their sons and sons' hearts to their fathers. We ask for skill, patience, grace, and the power of the Holy Spirit as we do this. I thank you for the time we've had together studying The Intentional Father, and I pray for changed generations.

In Jesus's name, Amen.

NOTES

Chapter 1: There Is a Need for Fathers

1. "The Proof Is In: Father Absence Harms Children," National Fatherhood Initiative, accessed November 3, 2020, https://www.fatherhood.org/father-absence-statistic.

2. Ronald Rolheiser, *Sacred Fire: A Vision for a Deeper Human and Christian Maturity* (New York: Crown Publishing Group, 2014), 26.

Chapter 3: A Preview of the Possible

1. Stephen R. Covey, *The 7 Habits of Highly Effective People: Powerful Lessons in Personal Change* (New York: RosettaBooks, 2013), 104.

Chapter 4: Honoring Your Father

1. Tom Wolfe, *The Bonfire of the Vanities: A Novel* (New York: Macmillan, 2002), 447.

2. Richard Rohr, "Transforming Pain," Center for Action and Contemplation, October 17, 2018, https://cac.org/transforming-pain-2018-10-17.

3. This is an adaptation of this thought from Jung: "An individual is infantile because he has freed himself insufficiently, or not at all, from his childish environment and his adaptation to his parents, with the result that he has a false reaction to the world: on the one hand he reacts as a child towards his parents, always demanding love and immediate emotional rewards, while on the other hand he is so identified with his parents through his close ties with them that he behaves like his father or his mother. He is incapable of living his own life and finding the character that belongs to him." C. G. Jung, *The Collected Works of C. G. Jung*, ed. and trans. Gerhard

Adler and R. F. C. Hull (Princeton: Princeton University, 1970), 284.

Chapter 6: Home

1. Alasdair MacIntyre, *After Virtue* (Notre Dame, IN: University of Notre Dame Press, 2007), 216.

Chapter 7: Values

1. Peter Kreeft, *Back To Virtue* (San Francisco, CA: Ignatius Press, 1992), 70.

Chapter 8: Five Shifts

1. Richard Rohr, *Adam's Return* (Chestnut Ridge, NY: Crossroad Publishing Company, 2017), 42.

Chapter 9: The Power of Preparing for Moments

1. Chip Heath and Dan Heath, *The Power of Moments: Why Certain Experiences Have Extraordinary Impact* (New York: Simon & Schuster, 2017), 63.

Chapter 10: Being Good at Being a Man

1. Dave Ferguson and Jon Ferguson, *Exponential: How to Accomplish the Jesus Mission* (Grand Rapids: Zondervan, 2010), loc. 1047 of 3988, Kindle.

Chapter 11: Roles to Master

1. Robert Lewis, *Raising a Modern-Day Knight: A Father's Role in Guiding His Son to Authentic Manhood* (Carol Stream, IL: Tyndale, 2007), loc. 836 of 2506, Kindle.

Chapter 14: The Gap Year

1. Wikipedia, s.v. "Liminality," last modified November 3, 2020, 19:38, https://en.wikipedia.org/wiki/Liminality.

Chapter 15: Ceremony of Welcome and Blessing

1. Dallas Willard, "The Right Way to Give Someone a Blessing," *Christianity Today*, January 8, 2014, https://www.christianitytoday.com/ct/2014/january-february/right-way-to-give-someone-blessing.html.

ABOUT *the* RESEARCH

RESEARCH FOR *THE INTENTIONAL FATHER* was designed and analyzed by Barna Group. Participants in the survey were U.S. men ages eighteen and older who have at least one biological child, adopted child, or stepchild between the ages of ten and twenty-five. The project was conducted online March 27, 2020, to May 7, 2020, and included representative surveys among 1,058 total respondents, including an oversample of 612 practicing Christians.

Barna wishes to thank the men who contributed their voices to this research, allowing us to gain a clearer picture of what's going on in the hearts of fathers today.

About BARNA GROUP

BARNA GROUP IS A RESEARCH FIRM dedicated to providing actionable insights on faith and culture, with a particular focus on the Christian church. Since 1984 Barna Group has conducted more than two million interviews in the course of thousands of studies and has become a go-to source for people who want to better understand a complex and changing world from a faith perspective.

Barna's clients include a broad range of academic institutions, churches, nonprofits, and businesses, such as Alpha, the Templeton Foundation, Pepperdine University, Fuller Theological Seminary, the Bill and Melinda Gates Foundation, the Maclellan Foundation, DreamWorks Animation, Focus Features, Habitat for Humanity, the Navigators, NBCUniversal, the ONE Campaign, Paramount Pictures, the Salvation Army, Walden Media, Sony, and World Vision.

The firm's studies are frequently quoted by major media outlets such as BBC, CNN, Fox News, the *Economist*, *USA Today*, the *Wall Street Journal*, the *Huffington Post*, the *Atlantic*, the *New York Times*, and the *Los Angeles Times*.

Barna works with leading voices in the church, such as Jon Tyson on this book, to help provide anchoring data and insights to their work. Also available are Andy Crouch's *The Tech-Wise Family* (2017) and Amy and Andy Crouch's *My Tech-Wise Life* (2020).

If cultural discernment is a kind of apologetic for faith, the Barna team is honored to help Christians understand the times and discover a faithful path forward in the way of Jesus.

JON TYSON is a widely respected pastor and leader in New York City and the author of several books, including *Beautiful Resistance*. Originally from Australia, Jon moved to the United States two decades ago with a passion to seek and cultivate renewal in the Western church. He has spent the last sixteen years pastoring and planting churches in Manhattan. Learn more at www.church.nyc.

Connect with
JON

@JonTyson